# Monuments of Bharatpur

Dr. Anil Kumar Verma

Originals

Delhi 110 052

First Published 2009



ISBN 978-81-8454-087-1

Published by
**Originals**
(an imprint of Low Price Publications)
A-6, Nimri Commercial Centre,
Near Ashok Vihar Phase-IV,
Delhi-110052
Phones: 27302453
e-mail: info@Lppindia.com
visit us at: www.Lppindia.com

Printed at
**D K Fine Art Press P Ltd.**
Delhi-110052



PRINTED IN INDIA

# Foreword

The Jats as a dominant agriculturist community operating in the north and north-western parts of the Indian Sub-continent, which on account of their natural and human resources and location played a crucial role in the political fortunes of the country. Similarly impact of the growth of Jat-movement in particular their militarization in Braj region had implications far beyond the region itself.

The Jat rulers were persons with vision who established not only socio-economic-politico structures but also left an everlasting legacy in the form of art and architecture. The monuments constructed by them are a reflection of their personal traits as well as their clan and society. The opulent lifestyle of Bharatpur rulers reflected in the palaces, fountains, lawns and tanks. The pleasure palaces of Deeg served as a summer resort for the royal families.

The contribution of the Jats to Braj culture can be noticed in the scenes of mural paintings in the monuments, particularly in the *chhatries* of Jat rulers ar Govardhan. The Braj culture which had been decimated by the muslim rulers was not only revived but also progressed in every sphere. The life–style of Braj people, their habits, their dresses, customs, festivals, their beliefs, their Gods etc. are depicted vividly in the *chhatries*.

Art and Culture flourishes after a certain level of prosperity has been achieved by the Society as a whole. This shows that the area where Jats dominated had a flourishing agriculture economy and that the Jat rulers were not looters or predators, as depicted by certain writers, but rulers who had wisdom and culture which resulted in the creation of magnificent structures and promotion of art activities.

Maharaja Surajmal ruled over Bharatpur which was comparatively a smaller state but his image as a wise ruler and diplomat was generally accepted.

These neglected monuments of Bharatpur State are at present in delapidated state. Like other forts of the State the imposing Lohagarh fort also is in ruins. The outer canal known as Sujan Ganga Nahar surrounding the fort has virtually become a septic tank.

The conservation of monuments–forts, gardens, palaces, tanks, dams, ghats, paintings etc. serves as an index of civilization. Monuments are the evidence of human developments in multifarious areas, ages and directions. They are precious since they further human knowledge regarding various aspects and spheres of our past life and therefore any loss to them is irreplaceable.

Keeping in mind the historical value and general decay of various monuments scattered throughout the erstwhile Bharatpur State, we requested Prof. Pritama Asthana, the then Head of the Department of History and Culture in Agra, later Vice-Chancellor of Gorakhpur University, through our honorary Director of Research and Publication to register this topic for Ph.D. in her department. She entrusted the work to her student Anil Kumar Verma.

I wish to acknowledge the serious efforts put in by Dr. Anil Kumar Verma in presenting this deep historical study on valuable monuments of Bharatpur State. I am sure this publication will be a useful contribution to the cultural history of later Mughal period.

Ram Niwas Mirdha

President

Surajmal Memorial Education Society

# Preface

'Some of the Jat buildings were so significant that the kind of these could not be found anywhere—not even in Delhi and Agra', said Ghulam Ali Naqwi, the author of *Imad-us-Saadat.* A visit to Bharatpur and Deeg proved how true it was. Bulk of literature emphasises on the narrative of Jat history on the traditional lines but none has tried to explore the hidden aspect of the character and personality of the builders reflected from the various monuments at Bharatpur, Deeg, Wair, Kumher, Vrindaban and other places.

My work is an exclusive study of the history of the Monuments of Bharatpur State. Surveying every nook and corner of the erstwhile State, I believe this study would open a new way for avid worshippers to explore more in this direction.

It is my pious and proud privilege to have worked under the supervision of a renowned scholar and historian Prof. (Mrs.) Pratima Asthana the then Vice Chancellor of University of Gorakhpur. Without her affectionate patronage and encouragement, this would could not have been completed in its present form. I submit my heartfelt gratitude to Prof. Agam Prasad Mathur, former Vice Chancellor Agra University, who generously provided me the fullest possible help in solving my problems.

I shall be failing in my duty if I do not refer to the encouragement and scholarly guidance which I have receieved from Prof. Sugam Anand, the then lecturer, Dept. of History, Agra College, Agra. My wife, Smt. Manisha remained a constant source of inspiration who lovingly persuaded me to complete this venture.

I am highly indebted to Sh. Ram Niwas Mirdha Ji, former Union Minister and President of Surajmal Memorial Education Society, New Delhi who inspired me to work on the Monuments of Bharatpur State. Sh. Mirdha Ji and Shri S.P. Singh, the then Secretary of the Society, rendered all help to me in completing this prestigious project.

I am grateful to Dr. S.S. Rana, University of Delhi who gave valuable suggestions about the references. Dr. Urvashi Dalal, M.D. University, Rohtak deserves my thanks who kindly has gone through the whole thesis and pointed out some blemishes in the language. I have tried my best to incorporate these suggestions while preparing the press copy. References of important works have also been updated with recent publications. I express my respectful gratitude to Dr. Vir Singh, Director, Maharaja Surajmal Centre for Research and Publication, who is not only my mentor but also one who rendered valuable help in the preparation of this work for publication.

For the sympethatic help in providing me the necessary facilities for work, I am also thankful to the librarians of B.R. Ambedkar University, Agra, Bharatpur State Museum Library, Hindi Sahitya Samiti, Bharatpur, Public Library, Bharatapur, Library of Archaeological Survey of India, New Delhi, National Archives, New Delhi and Surajmal Memorial Education Society Library, New Delhi.

My thanks are also due to the Publisher, *Originals* who managed the work in a perfect manner and brought the book in an attractive form.

Lastly, I dedicate this work to the sweet memory of my daughter Avantika( Akki).

Dr. Anil Kumar Verma

December, 2008

# Contents

# List of Plates

## List of Maps

Bur
Platfor
Chhatris -
Old building
Tank-I
Pillar – J
Gates – K
Tomb – L
Others –m

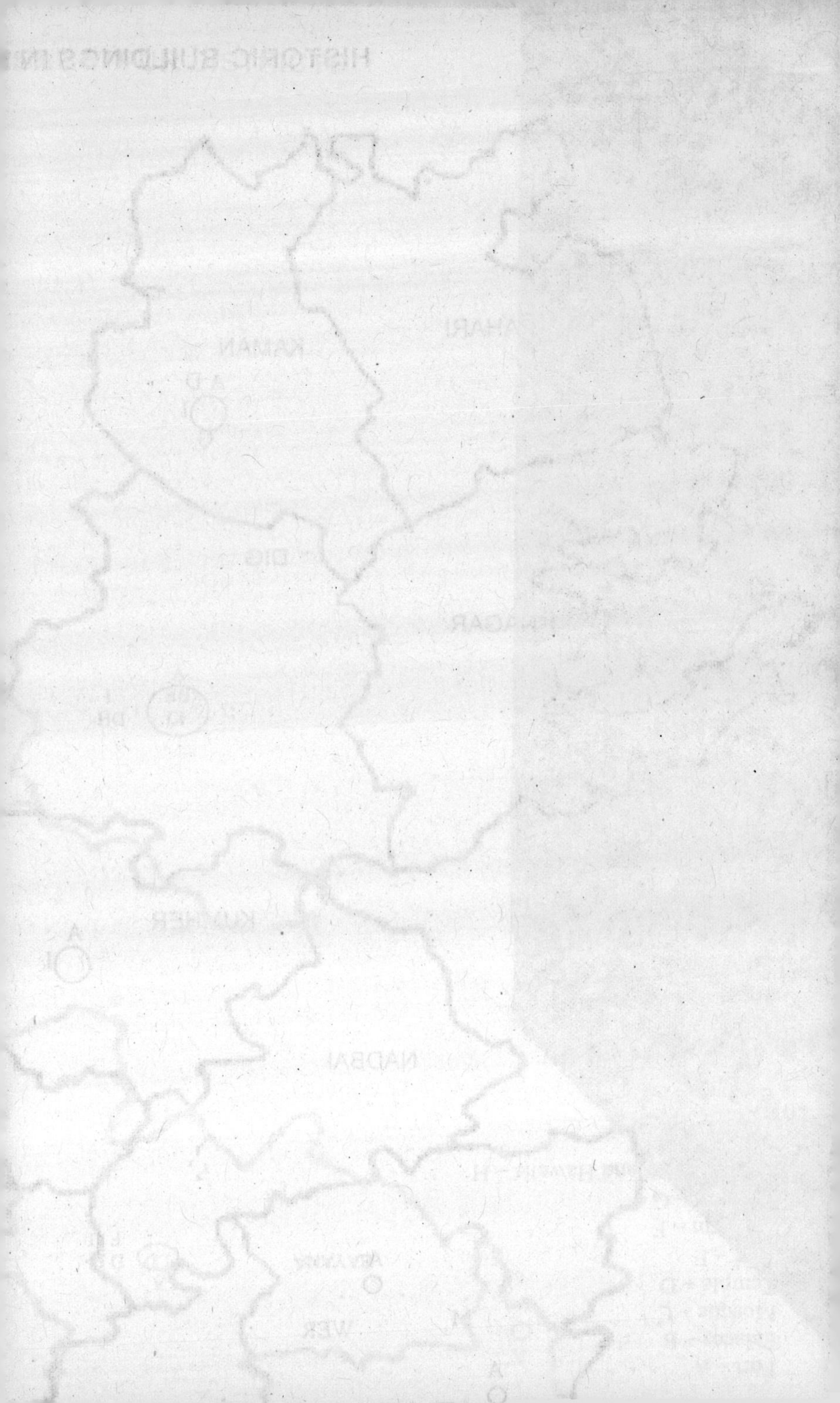

## *Chapter 1*

# Methodology and Sources

Methodology plays a vital role in determining the course of research. Use of modern techniques of historical research provide not only a framework to present a descriptive account of facts but also a scientific analysis of data collected from original and secondary sources. Historical research is an attempt to make a diligent and systematic inquiry or investigation into the subject in order to discover facts or revise the known facts or put the facts into theories because history is an integrated narration or description of past occurrences or facts written in a spirit of critical inquiry to find the whole truth.[1] Historical method is the induction of principles through research into the past and the social forces which have shaped the present.[2]

The facts with which history has particularly to do are the facts of record and these are indispensable not only for history in the narrower meaning of the word but also for every domain of science and art since an observation once made exists. Therefore, in the systematic accumulation and comparison of observation in any field of scientific study it is necessary to use or to rely upon the technical procedures of historical critius. Historical method is one step ahead as compared to the other methods like philosophical, institutional and legal. It attempts to explain as many points of views as possible and based on them draws generalization.

As far as scholars carrying out historical research are concerned, they are bound to differ from one another at all times and at all places. This is the result of all kind of modifications, considerations and view points. History thus, becomes, something dynamic. It moves with experiences contributing to an awareness which in turn leads to a modification both of circumstances and results. Keeping in mind the same objective Pt. Jawaharlal Nehru opined

1. P.V. Young, *Scientific Social Survey and Research*, p. 144.
2. *Ibid*, p. 145.

that "a blind reverence for the past is bad and so also is a contempt for it for no future can be founded on either of these. The present and the future inevitably grow of the past and bear its stamp and to forget this is to build without foundations and to cut off the roots of national growth. It is to ignore one of the most powerful forces that influence people...one of the present age has been the discovery of the past and the nation.[3]

Scientific historical research is dispassionate presentation of the past built on relevant proof. The touchstone of historical writing is its objectivity but history lacks absolute objectivity. Because the subject matter of history consist events or facts which happen at particular moments in time and then are no more. Moreover, the facts of history never come pure since they do not and cannot exist in a pure form. They are always refracted through the mind of recorder, hence, there is possibility of subjectivity in historical writings.

Research as a matter of fact, is a scientific undertaking which by means of logical and systematic technique aims to discover new facts, analyse their sequences, inter-relationships and causal explainations which are located within an appropriate theoretical frame of reference.

In the present work, research has been done on a scientific basis and main emphasis is laid on a critical assessment of historical facts. The monuments themselves are the most important living source, besides the relevant material which has been collected from archives, libraries, people etc. The works of contemporary or semi-contemporary writers have been consulted after a careful assessment of the nature and value of their works. Contemporary literature also provide valuable source of information to the present thesis. Literature, indeed, is a faithful mirror of a country's life for the period in which it flourishes. The prevailing ideas, tendencies and environment of a particular age are reflected to a considerable extent in literary works. Documents, journals, and books have also been consulted wherever necessary. The bibliography in this work contain detailed information regarding the sources.

Besides the primary sources, numerous secondary sources supply a good deal of information on the topic concerned. The opinions of learned scholars and historians cannot be ignored. The

3. Jawahar Lal Nehru, *The Discovery of India*, p. 627.

views of J.A. Devenish, James Fergusson, E.B. Havell, M.C. Joshi and F.S. Growse, who are considered as authorities on history of art and architecture, have also been analysed.

The mass of raw material which has been sifted and made to yield necessary results on scientific lines embodied in this research work may be placed together under four categories:

1. Monuments.
2. Literature
3. Foreign accounts
4. Inscriptions

## Monuments

The researcher has included the big forts i.e. Bharatpur, Deeg, Kumher and Wair, besides small garhies. The palaces at Bharatpur, Deeg, Vrindaban, as well as gardens, temples, ghats, dams and cenotaphs constructed by Bharatpur rulers are included in this work.

The researcher has tried to compile 'forgotten monuments' with the known monuments preserved by the Archaeological Survey of India. All knowledge gathered about the history and architecture of these monuments are given in the thesis to the best of the researcher's ability. Some of these monuments are living examples of national unity and integration in the country. Though some of them do not have any architectural merit yet they represent the emotional feelings of human hearts which can eradicate ill feelings which provide great obstacles in creating communal harmony.

The monuments throw light on the history and culture of the region in which they are located. They show that different religions were knitted into one and we could imagine the harmony with which they lived. Though not old, from historical and cultural point of view, the Bharatpur state was very prosperous.

Old people who had the knowledge of lesser known monuments are passing away one by one. There are a few religious places which are in a dilapidated condition. Most of the forts, gardens and tanks are bearing the same fate. They are in a state of destruction and decay.

## Indigenous Sources

This provides another important source on the history of the region and assists in the formulation of a hypothesis on the specific field of research. The researcher studied the contemporary sources and analysed them. Some of the main sources on the Jat history and architecture on which rests the entire plan of the researcher are as follows :–

1. *The Jats: Their Role in the Mughal Empire* by G.C. Dwivedi.
2. *Dig* by M.C. Joshi.
3. *Dig, its History and Palaces* by Jawala Sahai.
4. *Imad-us-Saadat* by Ghulam Ali Naqvi.
5. *History of the Jats*, by K.R. Qanungo.

Baring M.C. Joshi, an archaeologist par excellence, and Jawala Sahai, a *munshi* in Bharatpur State, rest of the authors have dealt with a broad field yet they throw some light on the history of architecture which has helped the researcher a lot.

## Foreign Accounts

These have always been an authentic source in knowing the history. The foreign travellers and writers are away from certain prejudices in which the court writers may fall. Though they are not so aquainted with the society and politics of the country yet they write what they feel. They are not biased and upto a certain extent their information can be regarded authentic. The researcher is lucky to find certain foreign writers who worked extensively on architecture including palaces of Deeg. One scholar is F.S. Growse who worked hard to explore the history of Braj region. Again J.A. Devenish is another great informer on Deeg. He was the executive engineer for the Bharatpur state. He was also the main architect of *Bundh Baretha*. Besides these, Frans Gottlieb Kuen known by his pen name Fransoo, Fergusson and E.B. Havell throw much light on relevant field which helped the researcher a great deal.

## Inscriptions

Inscriptions are another original source to know the history of a particular region. In the researchers case, he has been benefitted by them though they are not in abundance. Specially Bundh Baretha, temple at Bharatpur fort, tank at Agra are the places to which the researcher is indebted to the inscriptions which helped him immensely in the compilation of his work.

All the sources and few authorities on Jat history which the researcher consulted helped him to complete this entirely new endeavour in the field of the history of art and architecture of the Jat rulers.

The present dessertation 'Monuments of Bharatpur State' comprises a new field of enquiry - the study of Jat monuments from the time of Raja Badan Singh to Maharaja Brijendra Singh. It is an exclusive study of the history of Jat monuments reflecting the character and personality of the Jat rulers.

Some of the Jat buildings are so magnificant that the kind of these could not be found "anywhere - not even in Delhi and Agra" this statement of Ghulam Ali Naqvi, the author of *Imad-us-Saadat,* provoked me to delve into the subject and find out its worth.

After selecting the topic, the researcher prepared the list of monuments belongings to the Bharatpur State which are numerous and widely spread through the nook and corner of the Braj region, Rajasthan and in the Indo Gangetic plain. After collecting nearly all the living and faded monuments with the help of Archives, Archaeological Survey of India and consulting authorities on Jats in different libraries, the researcher selected a number of buildings and again categorized them into (i) Forts (ii) Palaces (iii) Gardens (iv) Tanks (v) *Chhattris* (vi) *Ghats* (vii) Mosque and (viii) Temples. After planning a central theme, keeping in mind the continuity and the promise of yielding specific conclusions the researcher has devolved on the history of selected monuments and in carving out the personality and character of the builders as revealed their construction.

After framing the outline necessary arrangements were made for collection of relevant and adequate data for the study. In historical research the investigator must deal with data that is already in existence. Therefore, sources of data were identified. While collecting data, the researcher went through all the sources available and prepared a note of the related facts. In collecting data three different kinds of notes were prepared. The first is bibliographical note in which the author, title, page, place, date of publication and other information about the documents are noted. In the second, the greater body of the subject notes are presented and the third are the method notes which contain the suggestive and interpretative notes.

In collecting material, the researcher had to pass through many hardships. There is bulk of literature on the narrative of the Jat history on the traditional lines but none has tried to explore the history of the monuments and the hidden aspect of Jat ruler's character and personality which is constantly reflected in the various monuments at Bharatpur, Deeg, Wair, Kumher, Vrindaban etc. Some books dealing with better known monuments of Bharatpur State helped a lot. In this connection, the researcher was impressed by the pioneer work presented on Deeg by Mr. M.C. Joshi, Director-General of Archaeological Survey of India. The researcher went through his book and personally visited that place in order to build up my base regarding the work. This experiment proved to be a great success. The researcher visited all the listed monuments one by one, not once but many a times and noted down my own investigations. The researcher has avoided to the best of his capability the prejudices in determining the personality of Jat rulers. The researcher went through the mural paintings, the strength of the structures, the architectural beauty and the vastness in order to estimate his result.

Secondary sources helped me to determine the history of the monuments. Though most of the sources contain political history but they give a clear picture of the battles, treaties and ceremonies that occurred in those places.

After evaluating the collected data and the work of criticism, the concentration was on the grouping of the facts. This grouping of facts in a systematic order through a scientific causal genesis is known as the synthetic operation. It mainly determines how to set bound to the subject, to classify it into various periods and finally to decide what facts are to come into the synthesis and what are to be rejected.

The researcher not only critically examined the monuments but also tried to compare them with other contemporary and past monuments. Because of the vast nature of the topic it was almost impossible to provide a comparative study of all monuments but the influence of the other cultures and the general nature of style and execution have been analysed. There were so many petty monuments which had to be left out because it was not possible to include the whole bulk in this thesis. To sum up, it can be said that in the present work research has been made on scientific basis and main emphasis is laid on critical assessment of the facts. I hope this work will not only enhance the knowledge of its readers but it will also open a way to the new researchers to explore more in this direction.

## *Chapter 2*

# Background of Bharatpur State

The capital of erstwhile Bharatpur State is the town of presently Bharatpur situated in the eastern most district of Rajasthan. It forms boundaries with Gurgaon district in the north; Gurgaon, Mathura and Agra districts in the east; Morena district of Madhya Pradesh in the south; and Sewai Madhopur and Alwar districts of Rajasthan in the west. The river Chambal forms the southern boundary with Madhya Pradesh. In shape the district is a flat bottomed and irregulary incised skewed, bizarre figure. The district lies between 26°22' and 27°50' north latitudes and 76°53' and 78°17' east longitudes.

This area occupies an important place in the cultural history of India. It was closely associated with the ancient kingdom of 'Matsya Desh.' During the 4th and 5th centuries B.C. the region covered by Bharatpur, Dholpur and Karauli formed part of the 'Surasena' Janapad with its capital at Mathura.

The close proximity of the district of Mathura in the east and to Bairath (old Virata) in the West lends to the area an antiquity of epic age when Matsya inhabited this region. This tribe is mentioned in the Regveda along with other Aryan tribes.[1] To be more exact, it then comprised the modern Alwar-Jaipur-Bharatpur territory with Virata Nagar (Modern Bairath) as its capital.[2]

The discovery of the minor rock edict of Ashoka at Bairath goes to prove that this region was included in the Mauryan Empire. The disintegration of the Mauryan Empire was followed by the invasion of foreigners and evolution of small principalities. After the fall of Pushyamitra and the end of Greek invasion in the closing years of the first century B.C., the rule of the tribal republics, Yaudheyas and Arjunayans appears to have emerged in the lands within the triangle,

1. Bhargava, M.L., '*A Geography of Rig Vedic India*', Lucknow (1964), p. 50.
2. Sircar D.C., '*Studies in the Geography of Ancient and Mediavel India*'. Delhi (1960), p. 105.

Delhi-Jaipur-Agra. This is corroborated by the discovery of an inscription of about third century A.D., of the Yaudheyas at Vijay Garh or Bijay Garh near Bayana.[3]

The Gurjars came into prominence about the second half of the sixth century and portions of this district fell within the ancient Gurjaratra of Gurjara country.[4] In the later period of the Pratihara supremacy Nagabhat II of this dynasty had definitely a hold on Matsya which is proved by the Gwalior inscription.[5]

In the ninth century a branch of the Chauhan family apparently as a feudatory of the imperial Pratiharas of Kanauj ruled in Dholpur.[6] Three chiefs of this family are known. They were Isuka, his son Mahisharama and the latter's son, Chandamahasena.[7] In 1170 A.D., the Yadu king Sahanapala succeeded Haripala. An inscription of Haripala dated A.D. 1170 has been found at Mahaban. Similarly an image inscription of the reign of Sahanapala Deva, dated A.D. 1172, has been discovered at Aghapur in the old Bharatpur State.

This region suffered the fury of Ghoride invasion and later on came under the control of slave rulers. After the death of Qutb-ud-din Aibak the hold of the Turks over this area weakened owing to the efforts of the dethroned rulers who were endeavouring to revive their power. Actually Mewat or the country of Meos which included the district of Mathura, parts of Alwar, Gurgaon and Bharatpur States, became an abode of notorious rebels and a source of constant trouble to the rulers of Delhi in the time to come.

It appears that parts of this area were under the sultanate of Ala-uddin-Khalji as well. During the reign of the later Tughlaqs this area became still more turbulent. With the passage of time Sayyed and Lodis who held Delhi kept on controlling most of the area. With the advent of Mughals this area permanently remained under their control in peace till the haughty reign of Aurangzeb began.

Unlike most of Rajasthan this area is populated by Jats who were indeed a bold peasantry, their pride in their country accustomed

3. '*The History and Culture of the Indian people*', Vol II, '*The Age of Imperial Unity*'. Bombay (1960) p. 166.
4. Sircar, D.C., '*Studies in the Geography of Ancient and Medieval India*', Delhi (1960), pp. 162-163.
5. '*The History and Culture of the Indian People*', Vol. IV-'*The Age of the Imperial Kanauj*', Bombay (1955) p. 22.
6. *Ibid.* p. 107.
7. *Ibid.* p. 108.

to guide the ploughshare and wield the sword with equal readiness and success - second to no other Indian race in industry or courage.[8] They settled in this region long before either the Rajputs, Mughals or the Marathas became the dominant powers. In governing the villages they appear much more democratic, less reverent for hereditary right and had a preference for elected headmen. This sturdy and peaceful race living under the very shadow of the imperial capital rose in revolt. One of the many causes may be sought in the changed nature and scope of the Mughals government under Aurangzeb which was detrimental to the democratic and tribal way of life of the Jat fraternity. With his accession the comprehensive nature of the state gradually yielded to a narrow and over centralized despotic regime, which was naturally antagonistic to the democratic and tribal outlook of the Jats.[9]

The economic cause was also significant in leading the Jat peasantry to rebellion. The exploitation by the revenue collectors increased with the passage of time. Mughal assignment system in its actual operation became "ruinous to the peasants and ultimately harmful to the interest of the Empire."[10]

Against all this it was natural for the Jats to show their resentment over the prevailing assignment system as agriculture occupied the uppermost place in their life. "To be Jat, is to be a peasant or ploughman"[11] is the testimony of the French missionary F.X. Wendel, who lived among the Jats and studied them for quite a long time. Modave, a keen French observer, who visited India (1774 to 1776) was extremely impressed by the industry and voluntary attachment to and skill in agriculture which the Jats of Bharatpur displayed. Modave, remarks, "The Jats are, in general, good men and would occupy themselves under arms ------- one thing in my judgement does honour to the industry of the Jats; it is that ------- the plain is not as much abandoned as might be imagined and the fields there are better maintained than one would have expected."[12]

---

8. Risley, '*People of India*', (1908), p. 8.
9. J.N. Sarkar, '*History of Aurangzeb*', I, Introduction, XV; Sarkar, '*History of Aurangzeb*' (Calcutta 1924) V, pp. 455-457, 477; see also III, p. 216, qouted by G.C. Dwivedi, '*The Jats: Their Role in the Mughal Empire*', (2003), p. 16.
10. Irfan Habib, *The Agrarian System of Mughal India*, (Bombay 1963), p. 318 f. Sarkar, '*History of Aurangzeb*', V, p. 452.
11. Wendel '*Memoirs on the Jat Power*' G.C. Dwivedi p. 18. (Eng-1991), p. 7. (Fr. Ms.), p. 3.
12. Modave's French account, trans, by Sarkar, '*Islamic Culture*', XI, (1937), pp. 387-388, quoted by G.C. Dwivedi, '*The Jats: Their Role in the Mughal Empire*' (2003), p. 20.

Mathura region, the birth centre of the Jat uprising, suffered heavily in Aurangzeb's reign. Aurangzeb appointed Abdun Nabi as governor who demolished a temple in the city and upon its ruins erected a Jama Masjid in 1661-1662. He also removed, the stone railing of the famous temple of Keshava Rai in 1666.[13] The religious susceptibilities of the Jat peasants were shocked by the destruction of Hindu temples of Mathura whose lofty spires seemed to mock the edifices of Agra.[14]

The Jat rebellion broke out in the Braj region under the leadership of Gokula, the *zamindar* of Tilpat. Although the rebellion failed it had considerable, though indirect, repurcussions upon the future course of the Jat history. It exposed to them the strategic flaws in their ways of fighting. The fall of Tilpat within a short span of three days pointed out the hopeless vulnerability of their defence and its corresponding implications.[15] Ultimately, it watered the newly-sprouted seedling of liberty in the heart of the Jats.[16]

They gradually changed their existing military methods. There developed an increasing tendency to build their strongholds in the fastness of dense forests capable of withholding the onslaught of a powerful foe. The usefulness of working under a united leadership thus sowed the seed of House of Bharatpur which blossomed far more quickly.

After crushing the rebellion Aurangzeb broke loose his fury upon the Jat people who were normally moderate, light hearted and not unmanageable unless of course while excited. Modave is emphatic in pointing that Bharatpur Jats "are in general good men" who follow their peaceful pursuits "not obliged almost always to keep themselves under arms."[17]

For a decade the Jats, though simmering with discontent, were constrained to remain quiet. The Jats were looking for a suitable opportunity to wither away the bitter memory of their ruthless suppression by the Mughal imperialists.

---

13. Sarkar, '*History of Aurangzeb*', III, p. 293; cited by G.C. Dwivedi, (2003), p. 23.
14. K.R. Qanungo, '*History of the Jats*', (2003), p. 21.
15. G.C. Dwivedi, '*The Jats*', p. 27.
16. K.R. Qanungo, '*History of the Jats*', p. 22.
17. Ibbetson, 102; Bingley, '*Sikhs*', pp. 91-94 quoted by G.C. Dwivedi, '*The Jats*', p. 30.

The first leader, fifteen years after the death of Gokul Jat, among the Jats was Brij Raj of Sinsini[18] (16 miles north-west of Bharatpur). Brij Raj and his brother, Bhajja Singh, organised their clansmen to defy the government authority by plundering passersby, royal caravans and army provision. In 1682, a Mughal contingent besieged his stronghold, Sinsini. The Jat chief somehow succeeded in sending away his women from the fortress but was himself killed alongwith his son, Bhao Singh, while defending it. Having fled from Sinsini the family of Brij Raj sought refuge in a small and obscure mud fort (5 miles from Bayana). Here one of the wives of Bhao Singh gave birth to a posthumous son named Badan Singh. It is after the name of this personage that the garhi is still known as 'Badangarhi.'[19]

Brij Raj in old age put Raja Ram, the son of Bhajja Singh, in charge of the anti-Mughal activities. Raja Ram proved a great rallying point and a great number of the Jats were united under his leadership. He gave them military training and equipped them with fire arms. He gave similar attention to the strengthening of his defence for which he built his forts (garhi) at advantageous positions, amidst the dense deep *jungles* of the Jat country and strengthened them with mud walls that could render them stronger to defy artillery. These forts served as basis for operations and refuge as also places for dumping the booty.[20]

Raja Ram's increasing disturbances worried the Emperor for he had ended the authority of the Mughals in the Agra district closing the roads to traffic and plundering many villages. An internecine war raged between the Shekhawat and Chauhan clans of Rajputs for lands in the Bagtharia and some other *paraganas*. The result was the battle in which Raja Ram sided with Chauhans. When the battle was in its full fury the gallant Raja Ram led a fierce charge against the centre consisting of their foe Mughals. Meanwhile a Mughal musketeer who had hidden himself in a tree fired RajaRamat his chest. He fell

18. '*Imperial Gazetteer*, VIII, 75; U.N. Sharma, '*Itihas*' I, 100 f; Sudan, *Sujan Charitra* (Kashi, ed.) cited by G.C. Dwivedi, '*The Jats*', p. 32.
19. *ODIER SETTLEMENTS REPORT, BHARATPUR*, referred to by Ganga Singh, *Yadu Vansha*, Vol. I, pp. 47-48; Somnath : *Dirgh Nagar Varnan*, (Kashi Nagari Pracharini, Hindi Ms) 3, *Ras Peeushnidhi and Madhav Vinod* in Somnath Granthawali (ed. by Sudhakar Pande, Kashi 1971 A.D.), 3, and 318, presents an exaggerated picture of the qualities of Bhao Singh, cited by G.C. Dwivedi, '*The Jats*', p. 33.
20. G.C. Dwivedi, '*The Jats*', p. 34.

down from his horse and died immmediately. His fall signalled the defeat of the Chauhans.[21]

Amidst the circumstances Raja Ram's aged father Bhajja Singh of Sinsini assumed the leadership of the Jats. Raja Ram's son Jorawar Singh worked as his deputy but he lacked in efficiency and resourcefulness.[22]

Fateh Singh, the other son of Raja Ram became the leader after the fall of Sinsini and the arrest of Jorawar Singh. But getting sceptical about his capabilities the Jats discarded Fateh Singh[23] in favour of Raja Ram's cousin, Churaman II, who was undoubtedly more capable than Fateh Singh. He had a genius for organisation and making clever use of opportunities.[24]

The departure of Bishan Singh and Shah Alam from the Agra province[25] in 1696 provided opportunity to Churaman to make up the losses, consolidate his position, and carry forward the work of Raja Ram. Within a short time the number of his followers increased to 14,000. Churaman built new forts in the impenetrable forests for the purposes of defence and preservation of booty. Among the new forts, he built a formidable one at Thun (11 miles to the west of Deeg) in a low marshy and thickly wooded tract.[26] Certain traits of his character suggests that as a person he was complex ambitious, bold and rapacious, Churaman II was cunning to an unusual degree. During his leadership the Jat power made rapid progress. The interest he evinced in training, equipment and expansion developed the Jat army into a reckonable force. Churaman, lacked that prudence, vision and spirit of accomodation which were necessary in a successful leader of a tribal and democratic people like Jats. But he did a lot for this race. He lost temper, because of the misbehaviour of his son Muhkam Singh committed suicide by taking poison.[27]

Muhkam Singh succeeded his father to the leadership. Ill tempered, domineering and pugnacious he was incapable as a leader. A majority of the Jat leaders apparently headed by Badan Singh

21. K.R. Qanungo '*History of the Jats*'. p. 24.
22. William Irvine, '*Later Mughals*', I, p. 322; G.C. Dwivedi, '*The Jats*', p. 41.
23. Drake and Brockman, '*Mathura Gazetteer*', p. 197.
24. Prof. J.N. Sarkar's article '*Jats and Gaurs*'-Modern review, October 1923 cited by Qanungo, '*History of the Jats*', p. 26.
25. '*Maasir*', p. 382.
26. '*Imad-us-Saadat*', Persian Text, p. 55; Wendel, '*Memoirs on the Jat Power*', p. 16; Shivdas, '*Shahnama Munawwar Kalam*' p. 19.
27. G.C. Dwivedi, *Tha Jats*, p. 83-87.

disapproved of him. Getting jealous of Badan Singh's bravery and ability, Muhkam Singh threw that chief into prison and reluctantly freed him after some time at the command of his guru, *Bairagi*.[28]

Jai Singh at last undertook the charge of subduing the Jats. Badan Singh who was with the army of Raja Jai Singh pointed out the weak spots and helped in the reduction of two fortified outworks. After conducting the defence for two months Muhkam Singh lost heart, and secretely fleeing from Thun, took refuge with his father's ally, Raja Ajit Singh Rathore.[29] On November 18, 1722, the imperialists entered the fort of Thun, demolished it, and had the site ploughed by asses. Badan Singh was installed as the chief of the Jats with the title of Thakur by the ruler of Jaipur.

It has been argued that Badan Singh "had to begin everything from the very foundation" since the work of Churaman left no trace.[30] It is true as far as his strongholds are concerned because they were raized to ground. The emergence of Thakur Badan Singh as the leader of the Jats marks the dawn of a new era in their history. It signalled the ascendancy of the forces of stable conquest and steady growth over those of dubious and erratic expansion.[31]

The task of Badan Singh was onerous indeed. He wanted to transform his princely insignia into the reality of a sovereign power. Fearing the possible Mughal opposition, Badan Singh began cautiously, combining coercion with conciliation, force with appeasement, and princely grandeur with humility. He raised a well-equipped force consisting of infantry and cavalry. In place of Sinsini, Thun and Sogar destroyed earlier he began erecting new forts at Deeg and Kumher, the foundation of former having been laid by Jai Singh.[32]

28. G.C. Dwivedi, '*The Jats*', pp. 88-89.

29. K.R. Qanungo, '*History of the Jats*', pp. 3-4.

30. J.N. Sarkar, '*Fall of the Mughal Empire*', II, 426.

31. G.C. Dwivedi, '*The Jats their Role in the Mughal Empire*', p. 95.

32. Wendel, '*Memoirs on the Jat Power*', pp. 20-24; J.N. Sarkar, '*Fall of the Mughal Empire*' II, pp. 428-429; Qanungo, '*History of the Jats*' pp. 35-37; G.C. Dwivedi, '*The Jats*', p. 97.

Badan Singh had some taste for beauty in art and nature which is testified by the remains of his numerous buildings and garden-palaces. He beautified the fort of Deeg with handsome palaces, which are known as '*Purana Mahal*.' In Bayana district, at Wair, he planted within the fort a large garden with a beautiful house and reservoirs in the centre called *phulbari*. He also built palaces at Kamar and Sahar which are now in ruins, and dedicated a temple known by the poetic name of *Dhir Samir*[33] at Vrindavan.

Having mustered sufficient power and wealth Badan Singh secretly started manufacturing arms and ammunitions. He fortified his lands, enlisted the help of his clansmen to whom he had given honourable places and also secured the help of almost all the communities in his role as a protector of the people against the corrupt rule of Delhi.[34]

Badan Singh raised the dignity of the Jat community in the country. He shaped the Jat State of Bharatpur and fulfilled a long cherished desire of this sturdy race to carve out a state for their own. This vision was fulfilled when the Mughal Emperor recognised Badan Singh as a 'Raja' in 1752. Wendel says : "This was the first step in the ascendancy of the Jats, because though they had before this acquired enough of goods and riches, they have not obtained rank among the potentates of Hindustan for want of title and authority; but now their head was created a Raja by the Great Mughal himself."[35]

The renewed efforts of the Jats in enlarging their dominion were quickly fructifying. At this juncture Badan Singh passed away at a very ripe age on 7th June,[36] 1756, leaving behind a Jat kingdom of his dreams, well carved. Badan Singh's death did not make much difference because his able successor, Suraj Mal, continued his lofty mission of raising the status of the community and to free themselves from the atrocities of Mughal and Rajputs.

Raja Suraj Mal, the successor of Badan Singh, was a strongly built man who possessed a steady intellect, great political sagacity and a clear vision. "Though he wore the dress of a farmer, and could

---

33. K.R. Qanungo, *History of the Jats*, p. 37; G.C. Dwivedi, '*The Jats*', p. 117.
34. J.N. Sarkar, '*Fall of Mughal Empire*', II, p. 317.
35. J.N. Sarkar, '*Fall of the Mughal Empire*', II, p. 312; also see, Wendel, '*Memoirs on the Jat Power*', p. 41.
36. K.R. Qanungo, '*History of the Jats*', p. 37 gives the date of Badan Singh's death 9th June; G.C. Dwivedi, '*The Jats*', p. 115.

speak only his own Braj-dialect, he was the Plato of the Jat tribe."[37] He was prudent and skilled, possessed all the noble qualities of his race, courage, energy, shrewdness and an indomitable spirit that would never accept a defeat. He was a wary old bird that picked up grain from every net without getting entangled in the noose.[38]

Besides the army, Suraj Mal also raised a network of fairly strong forts. The notable Jat forts built or repaired during his father's and his own period were those of Bharatpur (1743-1750), Deeg. Kumher, Wair, Ramgarh (Aligarh), Khurja, Kishangarh, Nimran, Thun (built on another site), Sinsini, Sonkh, Sahar, Sogar, Kama, Noh, etc.

So great and persistent was the popular trust in his benevolence and humane outlook that multitudinous people along with their valuables and families sought protection in his state in the face of recurrent threats. In 1761, on one occasion, the compassionate Jat spent as much as 10 lakhs of rupees from his pocket in looking after Maratha refugees.[39]

He was a great builder, and according to Wendel, spent "not lakhs but crores" on the magnificant edifices of the "truly royal" and "superb" palace of Deeg and the gorgeous fort of Bharatpur, both incomparable in Hindustan.[40]

At the time of his death he left to his successor, the standing army of 15,000 cavalry, 25,000 infantry, 300 pieces of cannons, 65 elephants and 5,000 horses besides not less that 25,000 well equipped soldiers posted in the forts.[41]

So long as he was alive Suraj Mal commanded the love, respect and admiration of his people. He handed down to his successor, a kingdom well cultivated, peaceful and out of the danger of being suddenly attacked.[42]

After the death of Suraj Mal the lowest order of nobility headed by Balaram, brother of Rani Hansia, proceeded to place Nahar Singh on the *gaddi* of Bharatpur as desired by the late raja. Jawahar Singh, the rightful heir to his father's throne and the eldest son took steps

37. *Imad-us-Saadat* (per. Ms.), p. 55.
38. K.R. Qanungo, '*History of the Jats*', p. 38.
39. G.C., Dwivedi, '*The Jats*', pp. 279-280.
40. Wendel, '*Memoirs on the Jat Power*', pp. 54-55.
41. *Ibid.*, p. 80.
42. *Ibid.*, p. 81.

immediately to check the likely challenge and despatched a letter to Deeg with a fast camel riding messanger conveying therein a stern warning to his brother and nobles, reproaching them with cowardice and unworthy scramble for gain. This was no season, so he would not claim at present his own birthright, but would go with the small force that remained with him against the enemy, and afterwards see who deserved most to succeed his father.[43]

Maharani Kishori, who wanted to see her adopted son succeed lost no time in turning the tide in favour of Jawahar Singh and appealed to the courtiers that she wanted nothing except to avenge of the death of her late husband so the *gaddi* should be given to the person who could avenge the death of their great Raja. This diplomatic exhortations of Jawahar Singh and Kishori captured the imagination of the Jat nobility. The next day when Jawahar Singh and Rup Ram Kataria reached Deeg they were received by due honour and Jawahar Singh was declared 'master and sovereign' of the State.[44]

Raja Jawahar Singh lacked neither the administrative capacity nor the soldierly qualities of his father. Apparently engrossed with the exciting game of war he was never remiss in his attention to the details of the civil administration or indifferent to the promotion of the arts of peace.[45]

Jawahar Singh, through his love of justice and strength to maintain peace, law and order and security from external invaders maintained the glorious tradition of his forefathers. Jawahar Singh's love of art and architecture can be seen from the edifices which were either renovated or constructed at his instance. He got constructed large reservoirs of water for boating and beautiful gardens intersected by canals fed by artificial fountains.[46] The other works being chhattri of Suraj Mal at Goverdhan,[47] Shri Laxmanji's temple at Wati (near Mathura), Shahpur (near Deeg) and the Deeg town itself. Likewise, he added Delhi Gate, Goverdhan Gate (Jawahar Burj) to the famous fort of Bharatpur and also constructed new palaces in it which are fine specimens of architecture.[48]

---

43. Wendel, *'Memoirs on the Jat Power'* p. 82; Qanungo, *'History of the Jats'*, p. 98.
44. Ram Pande, *'Bharatpur'*, p. 88; Rajpal Singh, *'Rise of the Jat Power'*, p. 159.
45. K.R. Qanungo, *'History of the Jats'*, p. 126.
46. *Ibid.*, p. 167.
47. M.S. Ranawat, *'Bharatpur Maharaja Jawahar Singh Jat'*, p. 91.
48. U.N. Sharma, *'Jaton Ka Navin Itihas'*, I, pp. 331, 337.

During his short rule (December 30, 1763 to first week of August, 1768), Jawahar Singh "extented the Jat possession to its utmost limit".[49]

The glory of the Jats departed with the death of Raja Jawahar Singh and confusion fell on their kingdom when his iron grip no longer held the tribe together. His younger brother, Ratan Singh, an imbecile and profligate youth succeeded him and reigned for ten months and thirteen days.[50]

The child, Kehri Singh, was seated on the *gaddi* after the sudden death of Ratan Singh. The half brothers of the late Raja Nawal Singh and Ranjit Singh quarrelled over the coveted office of regent. Nawal Singh being the elder had a better claim. The nobles kindled the flames of a civil war. French Captain M. Madec took the side of Nawal Singh and led an army against Ranjit Singh who had shut himself in the fort of Kumher.

Raja Nawal Singh paid dearly for his folly in rekindling the flames of war which did not subside even after consuming him to death, on Thursday, 10th August, 1775. Though he had disappointed his officers and troops at critical moments by his nervous timidity, they never ceased to believe that he would behave better next time. He did not possess such administrative ability and generalship. Nevertheless he was loved by his people for his friendly virtues and generosity and his death was sincerely mourned by all of them.[51]

On the very night of Nawal Singh's death the Ruhela mullah, Rahimdad, determined to try his luck by a bold piece of treachery. Having come to learn that the men inside the city had given themselves upto mourning and were neglecting the defence of the palace. Considering it to be the most opportune moment he secured entrance under the pretence of taking a mere stroll. He seated Kehri Singh on the *gaddi*, and got himself appointed his deputy.[52] A counter revolution was being planned against Rahimdad in the fort of Kumher where Ranjit Singh secretly assembled all the loyal chiefs of his tribe and intrigued with those in the city of Deeg for the expulsion of the usurping mercenary leader. One night Ranjit Singh started for Deeg

49. *'Imperial Gazetteer'*, vol. VIII, p. 76.
50. Qanungo, *'History of the Jats'*, p. 129.
51. *Ibid.*, pp. 130-31, 161, 163.
52. *'Ibratnama'*, M.S. p. 170, cited by Qanungo p. 164.

with a select body of troops. He and his troops executed their task with skill and bravery and falling unawares upon the Ruhela camp threw it into utter confusion. Within a short time he cleared the city of the Afghans, killing many and capturing a considerable number of them. Rahimdad fled towards Delhi and Ranjit Singh was installed at Deeg as raja in the place of his infant nephew, Kehri Singh, whose claim was set aside in view of the great danger to the Jat nation.[53]

Mirza Nazaf Khan had strained his energy and resources of the utmost in capturing Deeg in the belief that such a success would bring the Jats down on his knees. But the joy of the mirza turned into gloom when he found that in parting with Deeg the Jat did not intend to part with his independence.[54] Without suing for terms Raja Ranjit Singh prepared for a more obstinate defence of his remaining strongholds. Ranjit Singh made a good use of the short respite afforded by the embarrassment of Mirza Nazaf Khan at Ghausgarh. Ranjit Singh's hired Maratha troops who made a long night march and at early dawn fell upon the Muslim camp, immersed in sleep after midnight gaities. The Mughals fled more than 50 miles away without turning back till safe within the walls of Agra.[55]

Ranjit Singh, encouraged by this success, came out of Kumher and re-occupied the greater part of the territories lost by Nawal Singh. The Amir-ul-Umra out of the general good sent a letter to Ranjit Singh reminding him that there was yet time to secure pardon through submission and to atone for his past error by loyal service without dragging several thousand men into destruction. Ranjit Singh remained as haughty and obstinate as before.[56] In their hour of supreme peril they remembered the old queen Kishori who had out lived the glory of the house of Bharatpur. The well wisher advised him to send the queen to Mughal camp since she enjoyed the respect and good will of the high officers of the Amir-ul-Umra. But Ranjit Singh hesitated to act upon their advice lest the mirza should compel him to surrender unconditionally by detaining her in Mughal camp. One night, with his few followers, he escaped from Kumher leaving it to his fate. Rani Kishori fell a prisoner into the Mughal hands and was taken with all honour to the camp of the Nawab. When the Nawab

53. K.R. Qanungo, '*History of the Jats*', pp. 163-65.
54. K.R. Qanungo '*History of the Jats*' p. 177.
55. '*Ibratnama*' M.S. pp. 292-294, cited by Qanungo, p. 179.
56. '*Ibratnama*' M.S. p. 346, cited by Qanungo, p. 183.

Amir-ul-Umara learnt the distress of her his heart overflowed with kindness and he very graciously set her up as his own mother. He gave her the fort of Kumher for her residence and the '*mahals*' around it for her support. To please her he forgave the guilt of Ranjit Singh and left to him the fort of Bharatpur with territories worth seven *lakhs* of rupees as *jagir*.[57]

Ranjit Singh, the ruler of Bharatpur State, died in 1805 and he was succeeded by his sons Randhir Singh (1805-23) and Baldeo Singh (1823-25). The latter left a minor son, Balwant Singh, whose succession was recognised by the British Government but who was opposed and cast into prison by his cousin, Durjan Sal. The excitement threatened to end in a protracted war and the English decided to oppose the usurper and put Balwant Singh back in power. Lord Combermere invested the capital in December 1825 and Durjan Sal was made prisoner and deported to Allahabad. The charges of war were made payable by the Bharatpur State while the prize money (4,81,000) was distributed among the victorious army. Balwant Singh was installed as maharaja under the regency of his mother and the superintendence of a political agent.

Balwant Singh was put in charge of the administration in 1835. He died in 1853 leaving an infant son, Jaswant Singh. The regency abolished in 1835, was reestablished and a council was formed.

The uprising of 1857 had its repercussions over this region too. "Bharatpur, lying so near Agra, remained in a ferment of unrest throughout the Mutiny period. Great excitement prevailed in Bharatpur on the occasion of the mutiny at Mathura and the Bharatpur troops actually revolted. Major Morrison, under circumstances of great difficulty and danger, could carry on his duties till 8th July when he was ordered to quit it. Throughout the uprising Bharatpur had been in a position of great difficulty. Its territory was overrun by the mutinous soldiery. The citizens, inhabiting the native state of Bharatpur, had every reason to believe that the British empire was no more in India."[58]

Captain Nixon at Bharatpur volunteered to lead the troops of the state to intercept the rebel fugitives and maintain order. But two of his companies of Bharatpur troops mutinied at Mathura and the

57. K.R. Qanungo, '*History of the Jats*', pp. 183-84.
58. Khadgawat, Nathuram, '*Rajasthan's Role in the struggle of 1857*', Jaipur (1957), p. 72.'

Alwar troops were either bribed or overawed by the rebels so that they could take no action against the mutineers.

On March 11, 1862, 'Adoption Sanads' were granted to the rulers of Dholpur and Bharatpur by the British Government. It provided that 'on failure of natural heirs' the adoption by yourself and future rulers of your state of a successor according to Hindu law and to the customs of your race will be recognised and confirmed[59] as long as the rulers were loyal to the crown.

Maharaja Jaswant Singh, the ruler of Bharatpur, was a minor at the time of his accession. Major Morrison was appointed as political agent with full administrative powers. In 1858, a State Council was created. The ruler was granted full administrative power in March, 1871.

On the death of Maharaja Jaswant Singh in 1893 his son, Ram Singh, succeeded to the *gaddi*. He was by no means a popular ruler nor were the British Government happy with him. There were many unpleasant reports about his conduct. The English got an opportunity to act against him when it was alleged that he had killed one of his private servants at Abu. For this reason he was deposed in 1900 A.D. and Maharaja Brijendra Sawai Kishan Singh, born on 4th October 1899, was placed on the *gaddi*. During the minority of the new ruler the administration was carried on by the State Council. After the death of the ruler on 27th March, 1929, Brijender Singh (born on Ist December, 1918) was installed on the *gaddi* on 14th April 1929. Soon after on August 29, 1929, the ex-ruler Ram Singh expired. The young ruler was sent to England for higher studies as well as for reasons of health. On Ist November, 1930, a Council of State consisting of a president, five members and three secretaries continued to administer the state.

A political body known as the *Praja Mandal* started an organised political movement in Bharatpur (1938) which was declared an unlawful association.[60] This political body demanded responsible government under the aegies of His Highness, the Maharaja, and intensified its activities. Its members resorted to '*satyagraha*' campaign in April which continued till December 23, 1939, when it was

---

59. Aitchison, C.U., '*A Collection of Treaties, Engagements and Sanad's*', Vol. III, p. 35.

60. '*Report on the Administration of Bharatpur State*' (1938-39 A.D.), Bharatpur State Press (1940) pp. 4-5.

withdrawn after the settlement was reached between the Bharatpur and the *Prajamandal*. The name of the Prajamandal was changed to the *Bharatpur Rajya Praja Parishad* and its constitution, together with its aim and objects were revised. Then the organisation was recognised and registered by the state.[61]

The sentences of those convicted under the Criminal Law (Ammendment) Act 1937 for offences connected with the Praja Mandal Movement were remitted and the remaining political prisoners were released on the occasion of the '*Teej Durbar*' in August 1940.[62]

Then came the eventful year of 1942 when the Praja Parishad in Bharatpur also lined up with the rest of India and took to ways that led the State Government to pronounce their agitation "unconstitutional."[63] In September, the Praja Parishad suspended the '*satyagraha*' movement. The Government released all the political prisoners except two who had to be detained longer for special reasons.[64]

In October 1942 the government decided to set up a Representative Assembly in Bharatpur. It was known as the *Brij Jaya Pratinidhi Samiti*.[65] With a view to securing further public co-operation the ruler of Bharatpur announced on February 6, 1946, the appointment of a popular minister in the Council of State, who would be elected on the basis of adult franchise.

The time was ripe to attain independence and on 15th August, 1947, India was to get political freedom and all the prisoners in the *jail* were released on August 8.

As a result of the efforts of Sardar Vallabhbhai Patel the Matsya Union consisting of Bharatpur, Alwar, Dholpur and Karauli states was inaugurated on 17th March, 1948. Among the princely states of Rajputana this was the first union to be formed. The Matsya Union was merged with the united state of Greater Rajasthan on May 15, 1949 and with Rajasthan on 26th January, 1950.

61. '*Report on the administration of Bharatpur State*' (1939-40), p. 3.
62. *Ibid.*, p. 3.
63. *Ibid.*, pp. 3-4.
64. *Ibid.*, p. 4.
65. 'Brij Jaya coupled the names of his highness (Brijendra and her highness (Sri Jaya).'

## *Chapter 3*

# Architectural Legacy

Architecture not only provides a house or a palace to comfortably live in or temples, mosques or place of worship and devotion according to rituals and rites, or a *chhattri* or tomb to magnificently commemorate a departed soul, it is also a persistent and sincere effort to monu-mentalise the commonest and simplest things of the life of people e.g; a well, well-house or a step-well, a tank or reservoir, a quay or dam, a bridge, mile-stone, an inn, school and the like.

It is, infact, in such simple structures of daily use that the genius of people and potentiality of an art and the culmination of a civilization is best reflected. Each common place structure is a work of art, which may inspire posterity and invoke in it a feeling of wonder. The monuments of Bharatpur State reveal the minds, personalities and the conceptual framework and architectural skill of the Jat rulers who combined adventure with aesthetics, work with worship. The water constructions such as the Bund Baretha, Motijhil Bund, step wells, *baolies, sarais* and inns built by them though devoid of ornamentation appear as remarkable architectural achievements.

Though there had been a tradition of important chieftains among the Jats, the development of art and architecture started with the establishment of a strong kingdom by Badan Singh.

Jats 'are indeed a bold peasantry, their country's pride accustomed to guide the ploughshare and wield the sword with equal readiness and success-second to no other Indian race in industry and courage.'[1]

Scholars have traced the early history of the Jats to the epic age.[2] But this peaceful agricultural tribe came into prominence in Aurangzeb's reign when the changed nature and scope of the Mughal

1. K.R. Qanungo, '*History of the Jats*', p. 1.
2. '*Majmul-ul-Tawarikh*' in Elliot, '*History of India*' I, p. 104-105.

government[3] became detrimental to the democratic and tribal way of life of the Jat fraternity. Gokula, Raja Ram, Churaman were prominent chieftains during Mughal period. They all infused the spirit of unity among Jats.

It was during the leadership of Badan Singh that the idea of a separate Jat Kingdom came into prominence. Slowly and steadily he increased his power confirming the stability and peace at every step which is the very base for the development of art and architecture.

Badan Singh was a shrewd and crafty man who knew fully well how to avail himself of his opportunities. Fransoo tells us that he was "unrivalled in the art of a soldiery" and "possessed much proficiency in (the art of) spearmanship".[4] However, this skill does not quite accord with his general indifference towards military life as is obvious from his subsequent career as a ruler. Even as state affairs were mostly managed by his son, Suraj Mal, Badan Singh's main interest centered around non-military pursuits, namely, politics and diplomacy in which he showed himself quite adept.

The monuments constructed by Raja Badan Singh reflect expediency and his own sense of grandeur. With kingly power he sought kingly splendour as well. The palaces of Deeg sufficiently show the pomp, show and luxury with which Badan Singh led his life.

Badan Singh had numerous beautiful women in his *harem*, not inferior to the fashion of the country's great personages and the *rajas* of the time. The number of inmates of his harem slowly rising touched a prodigious mark. While Wendel puts it at more than 150 Fransoo carries it to "nearly 400 *ranis* as his wives.[5] Inspite of the assertion to the contrary by Fransoo the last figure very likely included concubines and maid-servants as well, as is alluded to by Harsukh Rai.[6] Because of his passion he constructed beautiful *Bhawans* to keep these ladies. The best example of it is the Hardev-Bhawan which was solely meant for the royal family. Besides it, he constructed a harem palace at Kumher, Kama and Sahar.

---

3. Sarkar, *'History of Aurangzeb'*, Vol. I, Introduction XII.
4. Fransoo, *'Tawarikh-i-Hunud'*, 14b, cited by G.C. Dwivedi, *The Jats*, p. 96.
5. Wendel's *'Memoirs on the Jat Power'*, p. 25; Fransoo, *'Tawarikh-i-Hunud'* (Pers, Ms.) 19a, quoted by G.C. Dwivedi, *'The Jats - Their role in the Mughal Empire'*, p. 97.
6. *'Majma-ul-Akhbar'* in Elliot, VIII, pp. 361-362,

Though it was Suraj Mal who was instrumental in giving a shape and design to Jat architecture, the credit of providing the infra-structure and political backing goes to Badan Singh. Being a shrewd politician he knew the importance of forts. Badan Singh could not tolerate even the strong castle of Soghar in his very neighbourhood. He ordered his son Suraj Mal to capture the fort which he did gallantly and successfully.

Raja Badan Singh was looking for a suitable site for a new capital. Sinsini was rejected because of inadequate water supply, Thun summoned unpleasant memories, so he finally decided to make Deeg his capital. The fort of Deeg was begun by him to protect him and beautiful water-palaces and gardens were built there.

Badan Singh was the master of the situation. The Lohagarh Fort at Bharatpur and fort at Deeg were two important and very strong forts. But the distance between the two was about 34 km. In the case of any siege or attack on any of the two forts the distance was considerable and it was not possible to come to assistance immediately. Sieges and attacks were the order of the day and Badan Singh's position was not stable. In order to send reinforcement at the time of need to capital Deeg and Bharatpur, Badan Singh chose a place Kumher which was in between Bharatpur and Deeg. Kumher is about 16 km. from Bharatpur and about 18 km. from Deeg. This place is connected by a metalled road which goes to Deeg from Bharatpur. There he built a fort besides many houses and a *Bhawan*.[7]

Badan Singh was a great lover of nature. The gardens at Deeg and a large garden at Wair shows his aesthetic sense and his fascination with the green natural surroundings. His efforts can be visualized as important measures to contain the desert.

Besides being a good statesman and leisure-loving he was a religious man. He built a temple at Vrindaban, known by the poetic name of *Dhir Samir*.[8] This temple is still standing at Kesi Ghat.[9] He liked the company of saints and followed their advice. On the

7. Fransoo, '*Tawarikh-i-Hunud*', 19a.
8. K.R. Qanungo, *History of the Jats*, p. 37; also G.C. Dwivedi, *The Jats*, p. 117.
9. This temple is totally renovated, the researcher was told that the temple was not built by any Bharatpur Raja, but the peculiar feature of the Jat architecture can still be seen. This is a sad aspect to belie the historical facts for personal benefits.

advise of a holy man called, Pritam Das, he decided to make Deeg his capital. Pritam Das was invited to the ground breaking ceremony. When he dug out eleven spades full of earth, Badan Singh said, 'Baba you must be tired, eleven is enough', Pritam Das dropped the spade and putting his hand on Badan Singh's shoulder said, 'For eleven generations your family will rule'. His prophecy proved remarkably correct.[10]

Badan Singh had at his command men, money and material. He had a keen insight into human character. He had able ministers to work for. Besides Rup Ram Kataria he had Jivan Ram Banchari who was quiet obviously a man of great ability and good taste. He appointed him as his minister of work to supervise his great architectural undertakings.

Art and architecture can flourish only with sound financial assistance and administrative back up provided by the resources of the kingdom. The land of the region of Bharatpur is noted for its fertility and productivity. On account of this the state had a rich source of revenue. Money came flowing from the taxes, land revenue and the possession of money looted and stored by the predecessors.

A large number of craftsmen, masons, sculptures and labourers were thrown out of employment due to the decline of the Mughal empire. They migrated from Delhi to the princely state of Bharatpur where they were engaged in the construction work. Cheap labour and enough money inspired Badan Singh to give a form and shape to his aesthetic dreams. The combination of Hindu-Muslim architecture of the Jat rulers is the outcome of their dedicated workmanship.[11]

Fortunately, the place of Bansi Paharpur and Baretha were in his empire ensuring abundant supply of marble and red stones for all construction activity in Bharatpur. The military might of the rulers was responsible for the uninterrupted entry of articles into Bharatpur which were essential and necessary to build the monuments.

The character and personality of Raja Badan Singh can easily be noted from the monuments he constructed. His death did not

10. K. Natwar Singh, *'Maharaja Suraj Mal'*, p. 22.
11. K. Natwar Singh, *'Maharaja Suraj Mal'*, p. 41.

produce any harm to the Jat kingdom because of his able son, Suraj Mal, who successfully took up the task upto his father's expectations during his life time. Suraj Mal contribution is associated with the major portion of Badan Singh's work.

Suraj Mal was blessed with a variety of military talents. He was a gallant soldier, an excellent tactician and "a great captain", as his great adversary Najib-Ud-Daulah himself admitted.[12] He was a worthy son of a worthy father. Though the credit of constructing the forts of Bharatpur, Deeg, Kumher, Wair, Ramgarh etc. goes to Badan Singh, but in reality it was Suraj Mal who really worked out these mighty castles. He was a practical man and well-versed in the mode of warfare. He so well designed the construction of Bharatpur fort that it was considered invincible before the advent of air craft. Even Lord Lake, one of the greatest generals of British Army, was not able to conquer it. So passionate was Suraj Mal in extending his empire and the reputation of his clansmen that he made his chief aim "to fortify Bharatpur so strongly as to make it absolutely impregnable and a worthy capital of his kingdom.....all the forts were put in a strong posture of defence, being armed with an infinite number of small pieces of artillery acquired by plunder or purchases and large pieces cast by himself."[13]

Suraj Mal had a remarkable sense of realism and military expediency. The fort at Deeg was originally intended to be built on the top of a pahartal, a mile westward to the town of Deeg. All the other forts in his empire were built on plains so he wanted to have a fort on hill to make it as strong and formidable as Amber. But it was on Jai Singh's intervention he decided to built the fort in the town on the plain.[14]

Suraj Mal was devoted towards his friends and respected those who did good to his family. He kept the words of Raja Jai Singh and constructed the fort at Deeg on plain. Inspite of his great wealth and fabulous riches he continued to show his respect to the Jaipur ruler Madho Singh till he was suspected of his motives. He left the Maratha camp because Bhau emphasized on removing the silver ceiling of the '*Diwan-i-Khas*' at Delhi. He said to Bhau "You have destroyed (the

---

12. *Nur*, 64b; quoted by G.C. Dwivedi, '*The Jats; their role in the Mughal Empire*', p. 281.
13. J.N. Sarkar, '*Fall of the Mughal Empire*', Vol. II, p. 137.
14. Baldev Singh '*Tarikh-i-Bharatpur*', Ms. pp. 27-28, cited by Ram Pande, *Bharatpur upto 1826*, p. 34.

sanctity) of the throne while I am present here and thereby brought odium upon me (as well). Whenever I make any request on any affair you disregard and reject it."[15] This clearly reflects the loyalty of Suraj Mal.

Suraj Mal was benevolent and popular and had earned people's trust and patronage. People along with their valuables and families sought protection in his state in the face of recurrent threats of war looting and arson. The upper storey of the Gopal Bhawan is still kept sacred to the memory of the wazir, Gaziuddin, who contributed, willingly or otherwise, the funds for the building of Gopal Bhawan and all the *bhawans*.[16] Surajmal spent more than 10 lakhs rupees to look after the Maratha refugees.

Suraj Mal had religious tolerance and he was as kind to Hindu as to Muslims. The abode of wazir Gaziuddin in Gopal Bhawan is a striking example of it. He had a humane outlook. Shamsher Bahadur came wounded from the battle of Panipat to the fort of Kumher; Suraj Mal tended him with utmost care; but he died in grief for the Bhau.[17] Suraj Mal had honoured the bones of a Muslim refugee by building a masjid and a house over his grave.[18]

Besides being a great statesman he, like his father, was a God-fearing man. His father Badan Singh sought his descent from Lord Krishna while he, himself, was his devotee. The Braj region is studded with the numerous religious shrines built by him. He is credited with building several tanks, arbours and temples in Govardhan, Vrindaban, Mathura and religious places. He and his successors are always remembered for their important contribution to the defence of the cultural and religious places of Braj region. The importance of Giriraj Govardhan increased under their patronage and several artistic '*chhattries*' were built along with other buildings.[19]

The successful expedition to Delhi of Maharaja Suraj Mal was commemorated at the Govardhan. He worshipped 'Haridev' and '*Deepdan*' was celebrated in *Manasi Ganga*. In the memory of this

---

15. Qanungo, '*History of the Jats*', p. 77.
16. Munshi Jwala Sahai, '*Dig its history and palaces*', p. 19; J.A. Devenish, '*The Bhawan or Garden palaces of Dig*', p. 10.
17. Sardesai, '*Panipat Prakaran*', p. 205.
18. *Imad-us-Saadat*, p. 203 cited by K.R. Qanungo, '*History of the Jats*', p. 83.
19. Drak and Brockman *Muttra Gazetteer*, (Allahabad, 1911), pp. 261, 321; also Growse, *Mathura A District Memoir*, p. 306.

expedition even now every year on Deepawali, '*Deepdan*' is celebrated.[20]

Suraj Mal was an obedient son. He fulfilled all the desires of his father. The foundations of all the four great castles were laid during the regime of Badan Singh. Badan Singh spotted out the places of strategic importance while rest of the work was entrusted on the shoulders of Surajmal to make them impregnable. He fulfilled the dream of his father by building up exquisite palaces and turning down the sleeping town of Deeg into a magnificent capital.

Suraj Mal, during the reign of his father, ensured a continuous flow of traffic on the highways passing through the sphere of Jat influence.[21] He took *parganas* of Khoh, Nagar and Kathumar in Mewat from Muhammad Shah for Rs. 2,40,000 per annum.[22] In 1738, he subjugated the lands of Ol, Farah, Achhnera and their neighbourhood in the Agra and Mathura districts.[23]

Except the khalisa parganas, the rest of the areas passed under the Jat control after 1739. Loose politico-economic controls had led to a stark decrease in revenue which increased only after Suraj Mal's take-over. Suraj Mal provided the Jat areas with a measure of peace and security from predatory raids and administrative oppression which the imbecile Mughal emperors had ceased to guarantee.

At the time of Suraj Mal's death the possessions of the Jats consisted of the districts of Agra, Aligarh, Dholpur, Etah, Hathras, Mainpuri, Meerut, Rohtak, Farukhnagar, Mewat, Rewari, Gurgaon and Mathura apart from the original principality of Bharatpur. The right bank of the Ganges forms the eastern boundry of the Jat kingdom, the Chambal the southern, the *subah* of Agra included in the territory of the Raja of Jaipur the western, and the *subah* of Delhi the northern, its length being about 100 *kos* east to west and 70 kos north to south.[24]

As regards the finances of the state, Father Wendel says, "opinions differ on the subject of the treasure and property which Suraj Mal left to his successors. Some estimate it as nine crores,

20. '*Braj Vaibhav*', editor-Gopal Prasad Vyas, p. 152.
21. *Sujan Charitra*, p. 10.
22. *Sujan Charitra*, p. 6.
23. *Agra Gazetteer*, p. 161; Drake and Brockman, *Muttra Gazetteer*, pp. 198-99.
24. K.R. Qanungo, '*History of the Jats*', pp. 95-96.

others less. I have enquired into his annual revenue and expenditure from men who managed them, all I could learn as more credible is that all his expenses were not above 65 lakhs a year nor below 60, and that he had, at least during the last 5 or 6 years of his reign, not less than 175 lakhs of revenue annually. He added 5 or 6 crores of silver to his ancestor's treasure....Today (after the accession of Jawahar Singh) upto 10 crores are in the treasury of Jats....much is buried - not known where. Suraj Mal fruitlessly dug at Deeg a large tract of land to recover part of the hoard of Badan Singh. This activity has given that city a tank and citizens have thus got water to their advantage."[25]

Years have not at all affected - but rather magnified - the popular belief about the fabulous wealth of the House of Bharatpur. Legends have it that the secret vaults of Suraj Mal's treasury still contain many rarities and choice plunder of Delhi and Agra which few can hope to see.[26]

The next ruler, Raja Jawahar Singh, possessed great military talents and administrative capacity. He could defy everything in the pursuit of ambition and revenge. He revolted during his father's regime and assumed the kingship after his death. Though his ambition superceded his affection towards his father for a short span it was he who put his life at stake to revenge the death of his father. His love and affection towards his father is depicted from the magnificant *chhattri* of his father at Govardhan.

Jawahar Singh had aesthetic taste like his father and grand father and built a *baradari* and *hammam* on Jawahar Burj and Jawahar Gunj at Deeg. He was a religious man and liked the company of saints like his father. It is said that Jawahar Singh's guru, Ram Krishan Mahant Bairagi (who often shared the charge of the Jat vanguard in the battles)[27] was guru of Surajmal also.[28] Being religious in nature he constructed a holy eight-fold chandra sarovar near Govardhan at Parsoli. This place was the devoted spot of Mahaprabhu Vallabhacharya and *bhakt kavi*, Surdas.[29]

25. Wendel, '*Memoirs on the Jat Power*' pp. 77-78.
26. K.R. Qanungo, '*History of the Jats*' p. 96.
27. *Nur*. 77a. He however, does not speak of the above Mahant being the Guru of Suraj Mal also; quoted by G.C. Dwivedi, '*The Jats*', p. 280.
28. Danadhyaksh family papers, quoted by Ganga Singh, '*Yadu vansh*', pp. 263-64.
29. '*Braj Vaibhav*', editor-Gopal Prasad Vyas, p. 152.

His successor, Raja Ratan Singh, was an imbecile and profligate youth and was extravagant. He was a follower of Lord Krishna and most of the time in his short reign he lived at Vrindaban where he was killed by a Gosain named Rupanand.[30] Near the temple of Madan Mohanji is the unfinished *chhattri* of him. After his assasination this cenotaph was left untouched and today it is filled with filth. The architectural instinct of his forefathers was present in him. He constructed *Panch Dwara* and *Topkhana* at Jawahar Burj.

Later Jat rulers, though always in a state of turmoil, kept on adding gems to their kingdom according to their likings. Balwant Singh was a man of religious tolerance. He devoted himself for the unity of Hindu and Muslim subjects of his kingdom. Ganga Mandir and Jama Masjid was constructed by him. By his order the Hindu and Muslim employees of the state had to give their first salary for construction to these religious places according to their religion.[31]

A very striking and characteristic feature of Jat rulers was their affection towards parents and brothers. Raja Randhir Singh's cenotaph was erected by Raja Baldev Singh who later ascended the throne. The cenotaph of Raja Baldev Singh was erected by his son Raja Balwant Singh whose own magnificant cenotaph was erected by his son and successor, Raja Jaswant Singh. The bunch of cenotaphs i.e. Suraj Mal, Jawahar Singh, Balwant Singh, Baldev Singh, Randhir Singh on the holy place of Govardhan shows the piousness, devotion and affection of the Jat rulers for their kinsmen.

They were not only generous to their dears but to the subject also. Maharaja Ram Singh completed the dam of Bund Baretha started by Maharaja Jaswant Singh to catch the flood and to employ maximum number on work during the scarcity.

Not only the Jat rulers were good builders, but their wives were ahead of them in this field. The foremost name is that of Rani Kishori. The queens were religious and lover of nature. The Braj region is studded by their constructions.

Mostly all the queens of Bharatpur house had aesthetic taste and devotion. Rani Kishori built many temples here and there in the empire. She constructed temples at Govardhan, Vrindaban and Agra. She also built Kishori Ghat at Vrindaban. She got built for herself a

30. K.R. Qanungo, '*History of the Jats*', p. 130.
31. G.C. Dixit, *Brijendra Vansh Bhaskar*, p. 182.

beautiful palace in the fort of Bharatpur. Rani Hansia, another consort of Maharaja Suraj Mal also built a *ghat* and garden at Mathura.

Rani Ganga, another queen of Suraj Mal, and mother of Ranjit Singh, who hailed from the village of Bachamadi built a beautiful palace or haveli at Vrindaban known as Ganga Mohan Kunj. This palace is unique in its elegant designing, massive pavilions and mural paintings.

Rani Laxmi, wife of Raja Randhir Singh, also constructed a *kunj* at Vrindaban. It is a mansion of high architectural merit. In the past many Europeans have praised the monument. Situated on the bank of river Yamuna it might well have served as a place where the religious minded queen worshipped.

The Jat style of architecture is mainly represented by the forts, mansions, cenotaphs and religious buildings. The structural elements, including the romantic landscape at Deeg, are basically the same as those forming the style of Shah Jahan, the Mughal emperor.[32] Therefore, formality, balance and symmetry are the essentials of this architecture. Besides it, the Jat rulers had a little but unavoidable traditional and environmental influence of the soil of Rajasthan in their minds.

The buildings are of entirely secular order. The palaces at Deeg and Laxmi Kunj at Vrindaban are marked by sophistication, regularity based on an order, and profuse and delicate carvings besides their double roof, emphasized on the exterior by lower and upper eaves. The characteristics of other mansions, like Badi Kunj at Vrindaban, Kishori Mahal at Bharatpur Fort, Purana Mahal at Deeg are, massive-ness, less systematic and less attractive internal arrangements and relatively simpler type of plastic decoration in brackets and pillars.

The material used for the construction was stone, brick, rubble and mortar. The red sandstone and marble are rarely used. Most of the buildings are of pinkish colour or finely plastered.

The Jat architecture is primarily of trabeate order. The use of arcuate system has also been made in certain instances. The arcades are of a decorative quality as each arch is formed by joining two

32. M.C. Joshi, '*Dig*', p. 6.

spandrel shaped slab cantilevers projecting from the pillars.

The general features of this style are engrailed arches resting on ornate pillars, flat roof-terraces, balconies and pavillions with Bengal roofs, hypostylar halls, double eaves, spacious internal arrangements and moderate structural height.[33]

Other attractions of the structures are pillars with floral bases, projecting dripstones, and tapering shafts normally surmounted by capitals bearing exquisitely carved flower-petals. The ceilings are generally flat though the domed and curved ones are also met with in certain cases. Amongst other varieties of arches the use, though limited, of semi-circular, trefoil and pointed apses too is worthy of note.[34]

Although not bearing a very imposing character, the palaces possess delicacy and dignity. This aspect of the structure never obstructs the unity of the conception. Yet on the other hand it strengthens the harmony between architecture and gardens.

To make the forts impregnable Suraj Mal prepared a threefold line of defence. These forts are unique in India from the point of view of durability, toughness and inaccessibility. Their ingenious design gave it an awesome reputation. On account of the indigeneous style of protective and offensive aspects and queer design, the Jat architecture is unique in itself throughout the northern region.

The striking characteristics of these forts are threefold line of defence, thick mud-walls, high perpendicular and steep towers, deep gorge, ceiling at greater height, and proper arrangements for cross ventilation all forming a confluence of durability, toughness and inaccessibility.

Thus, we can see that the Jat rulers cannot be dismissed as militant agriculturist crusaders whose only object was to amass material wealth. They indeed ruled with a vision which meant establishing not only a politico-economic structure but also leaving an everlasting legacy of art and architecture. The monuments they had built are a reflection of their personal traits as well as the nature of their society and clan and their political apparatus.

---

33. M.C. Joshi, '*Dig*', p. 8.
34. *Ibid.*, p. 8.

## *Chapter 4*

# Forts and Garhies

## Forts

The entire land of Hindustan is studded with imposing forts. The kings ruled from them and lesser chiefs built them to show their prowess. Right from the dawn of civilization the human being had had an instinct of his own survival and protection against natural calamities, wild animals and other rival agencies etc. This feeling initiated the need of shelters by raising obstacles etc. around their dwellings. To construct ramparts and fortifications around his residence might have been an earliest creation of humans. Recent archaeological excavations and studies have yielded ample evidence to prove the existence of forts and fortifications around the villages and towns of pre and protohistoric period which are further substantiated by evidences from literature.

Gradually the construction of ramparts, forts and fortifictions played a significant role in making history. In the constant struggle for power, forts and fortified settlements were a potent symbol of authority. Forts were the measure of a monarch's strength.

The forts were not simply inanimate buildings serving a military purpose; they housed some of the magnificant palaces ever built. They were alive and echoing with the sounds and symbols of some of the great dynasties, were witness to regicides and bloody succession battles and carried within their bastions harems and glitter unsurpassed. Thus, when writing the history of any era or of any empire it is the forts of that period which dominate the rise and fall of fortunes.

Before discussing the forts of Bharatpur State it is necessary to refer to ancient literature which provide us sufficient information about the technique of raising '*durg*', the Indian terms for forts, for defensive purposes. The Rigveda firstly mentions about the forts made of Aśmamayt (stone), the siliceous type[1], about the Ayasi (iron)

1. *Rigveda* II, 30.20 and *Rigveda* II, 35.6.

the metallic type[2], and about the '*Satabhuji*' forts (with hundred walls).[3]

The Yajurveda Samhita mentions the word Mahapura which means a great fortress.[4] The Atharvaveda too points out about the *vapra* (a rampart).[5]

The later Brahmanical texts like 'Upanishadas' refer to the word *Mahapura* and *Pura*. The records of Magasthenes and the Pali texts focus on the use of wooden sleepers in the walls of the town of Pataliputra.[6] Apart from these texts, epics like the Ramayana[7] and Mahabharata, Manu Samhita and Brahmāṇḍa Purāna shed ample light on the forts and fortifications along with its different essential parts.

Panini refers to the *prākāra* (rampart), *Parikhā* (moat) and *dwāra* (gate) as important parts of the city for defences. Kautilya in his Arthasastra has described a number of forts to be raised on certain places in different localities namely *sthāniya kharvatika*, *dronamukha, sañgrahaṇa* etc.[8] He suggests that in all the quarters of the kingdom there should be defensive fortification. He adds the names of *audak* (water-fort), *antardvipa* (island-fort) - a fort in a place surrounded by low ground in which water is stagnated by *prastara* (rocky tract) or a fort in a valley in the midst of hillocks, a *dhanavana* (a desert fort) i.e. a fort in the wild country devoid of water and even thicket of soil in a sterile desert, *vanadurga* (a forest fort).

A number of texts have been written about the kinds and *Vastuvidya* (the art of architecture) which cover the buildings of *durgs*. These include the (a) *Narada Shilpashastra* (b) *Maurya* (c) *Aparajita prichha* (d) *Vasturaja Ballabha Vastumandane* (e) *Vastumanjari* and *Mayamata*.

About the types of the forts Vishwakarma's *Vastu Śāstra* describes twelve types of forts namely - *Giridurga*, *Vanadurga*, *Jaladurga*, *Irinadurga*, already mentioned by Vishnu Sharma. The

---

2. *Rigveda*, I, 38.8; II, 20.8; IV, 27.1; VII, 3.7; 15.4; 95.1; X, 101.8.
3. *Ibid.*, I, 156.8; VII, 15.4.
4. *Ibid.*
5. *Atharvaveda*, II, 71.1; Whitney's translation of Atharvaveda Cambridge Mass (1905), pp. 435-36.
6. *Strabo*, p. 702, *Arrian and the Mahapari Nibbanasutta*, p 120 ff also Davids *Buddhist India*, p. 262.
7. P.K. Acharya, *Encyclopaedia of Hindu Architecture*, Delhi (1978), p. 250.
8. These fortesses were raised in the centre 800, 400, 200 and 100 villages, respectively.

*Kūrma Durga* (Tortoise type) probably intented to trap the enemy. The *Ekamukha-Durga*, *Dwimukha-Durga* and *Chaturmukha-Durga* built on the river or the sea-coast were provided with one, two, three or four gates respectively. The tenth type was *Prabhā-Durga* having strong defences with several *prakaras*, guards, watchtower etc.. The eleventh type is known as *Parvata-Durga*-it was for the use of protection in a fierce battle. The last fort that he explains is *Ayudha Fort* which was well equipped with all structures and weapons necessary for both offence and defence purposes.

The author of *Yuktikalpataru,* King Bhoja Parmar, who was a great military commander and expert in designing forts, divides them into two types *Akritrim* (natural) and *Kritrim* (artifical). By the natural fort he meant the forts having natural defences and the artifical forts having ramparts and parapets built by human agencies. The contemporary text, *Mānasāra,* gives further details about the classification of the forts which were based on the situation and distribution throughout the kingdom which are as follows : (1) *Śivira* (2) *Vāhinīmukha* (3) *Sthāniya* (4) *Dronamukha* (5) *Vardhaka* or *Saṁvidhāna* (6) *Kalaka* (7) *Nigam* (8) *Skandhāvarā.*[9]

The *Akshabhairava*, a text of 16th century A.D. gives more details about the planning of the forts in its 21st and 27th chapters. Another contemporary text, *Devadhanya-Vilāsa,* also supplies informations about the forts.[10]

The science of forts and fortifications in mediavel times was so advanced that the *Silpaśāstras* mention not less than 19 forms of forts with different defensive scheme.[11]

We can sum up the kinds of forts basically into six types :

(a) The *Dhanva Durg* or Desert Fort - also known as *Nirudak* or *Maru Durga,* situated in desert, corresponded to *Arina* or *Mayamatta* like Kumher Fort between Bharatpur and Deeg Forts. The second category, *Airina,* used to be built of soil made barren by salinity. For example the fort of Jaisalmer (Rajasthan).

9. A.P. Singh, *Forts and fortifications in India*, Agam Kala Prakashan, Delhi, 1987, p. 64.
10. B.B. Datta, *Town Planning in Ancient India*, Delhi. 1977.
11. A.P. Singh, *Forts and Fortifications in India*, Delhi, 1987, p. 65.

(b) The *Mahi Durg* or Mud-Fort: It is classified into three sub categories-*Parighā*, *Pañka* and *Mṛd-durga*. The fort, embattled by mud-rocks, bricks and stones, was known as *Parighā* whereas the fort with a tract full of saline mire or quicks was known as *Pañka-Durg* while the *Mṛd.-Durga* might be having mud walls. The example of such fort is Bharatpur fort.

(c) The *Jala Durg* or Water Fort: These forts are difficult to access. They can be divided into two sub categories (i) *Antardvīpa* (Island Fort) and (ii) *Sthala Durga* (Land Fort). They get this name from the natural situation i.e., between the rivers and seas, where they are situated. The best examples of *Antardvipa* and *Sthala Durg* are Kaveripattanam and Agra Fort respectively.

(d) The *Giri Durg* or Hill Fort: These forts are built on a high mountain, much above the plain where the natural drop-errs from the vertical, the rock is scraped to make them unscaleable. The best example is Gwalior Fort. Another category of such fort is technically known as '*Guha*' (cave), of which Udaipur fort is a fine example of this type.

(e) The *Vriksha / Van Durg* or Forest Fort: These forts are surrounded by thick forests making them completely impregnable. They are further divided into two subcategories (i) *Khañjana* (ii) *Sthambha*. The fort hemmed in by fens variegated with thickness and thorny shrubs were known as *Khañjana* Forts while a fort surrounded by jungle of lofty trees but deviod of water is called *Sthambha* Fort.[12] Best example of *Khañjana Durg* is Thun Fort of Churaman.

(f) The *Nra Durga* or fort protected by men: This type of fort was based entirely on the manual strength.

One of the most crucial requirement of a fort was a regular supply of water to ensure self sufficiency during a siege which could last for months. The planners in the past gave great thought to the availability of this life saving element by laying down guidelines on storage and efficient reservoir elements. The source of water was a closely guarded secret to prevent the unscruplous enemy from poisoning it. Varamihra states that artries of flowing water lie at various depths beneath the surface of the earth and these can be located by on understanding of topography and environment.[13]

12. A.P. Singh, *Forts and Fortifications in India*, Delhi, 1987, p. 65.
13. Varamihra, *Brihat Samhita*.

However, where natural resources of water were scarce, as in the case of forts in the Rajasthan desert a common method of storing rain-water in tanks was deviced.

The rulers of Bharatpur constructed many big forts beside the large number of mud forts. Maharaja Suraj Mal, the anchor ruler of Bharatpur State, raised a network of fairly strong forts. The notable Jat forts built or repaired during his father's and his own period were those of Bharatpur (1743-50), Deeg, Kumher, Wair, Thun, Sinsini, Sonkh, Sogar, Sahar, Kama, Alwar, Noh, Jwara, Khair, Ramgarh (alias Aligarh), Ram Ghat, Kishangarh, Nimran, Aring, Khurja etc.[14]

Suraj Mal was a great builder and according to Wendel spent 'not lakhs but crores' on the gorgeous fort of Bharatpur, incomparable in Hindustan.[15] Besides emphasizing their splendour the forts served to strengthen their defences. These forts were strongly fortified, profusely strored and well garrisoned especially that of Bharatpur, Deeg, Kumber and Wair were wonderful creations of the native genuis. Their mud ramparts, coated with bricks and rocks were incredibly formidable in dimension while the ditch around was very wide and dug so deep that water burst up. Yet, another rampart, probably the city-wall, surrounded them at a distance of 'two or three kos', followed by '*marhalas*', at a distance of one 'kos'. Apart from their strong garrisons and big and small cannons atop, these strongholds contained immense supplies of food, fodder and ammunitions, '*ban*', lead and gun powder sufficient to last for years together without requiring any external aid whatever. The walls specially of Kumher and Deeg were literally lined up with cannons atop. All this had rendered these forts quite impregnable.[16]

The contemporary authorities have bestowed lavish praise on the marvellous strength of the Jat forts. To quote a few, an eye witness says that no other places in India contained such enormous provisions as did the Jat forts. He adds that no power in Asia had the capability to capture by assault these impregnable forts.[17] Their builder, Suraj

14. *Sujan Charitra*, 212 to 213; TAH., 1096; TAL., 220; Wendel, *Memoirs on the Jat Power*, pp. 23, 33, 49-50, 54-55, 68, 122-24, 125. *Tawarikh-i-Hunud*, 20b, 22b; Somnath *Ras peeushnidhi* Somnath, 6 to 7; *Nur*, 32b 6-b; *Imad-us-Saadat* 84; *Siyar*, IV, 27-28.
15. Wendel, *Memoirs* on the Jat Power, p. 54, 123.
16. *TAL* : 215; Wendel, *Memoirs on the Jat Power*, pp. same as in f.n. 14 above; *Siyar*, IV, 27-28 *Sujan Charitra*, 222; *TAH*, 1096; *Majma-Ul-Akhbar in Elliot* VIII, 361; U.N. Sharma, *Jaton ka Navin Itihas*, II, p. 251-53;
17. Wendel, *Memoirs on the Jat Power*, p. 122-23.

Mal, on inspiration of his father emphasized the same thing by proudly likening them with 'Alexander's Rampart'.[18] In the eyes of Ghulam Hussain Khan nothing short of a complete volume could do justice to the descriptions of the Jat fortifications or the means of their defence.[19]

Besides constructing the impregnable forts like Bharatpur and strong forts like Deeg, Kumber, Wair, the rulers of Bharatpur constructed and protected innumberable *garhies* or mud-forts scattering at every nook and corner of their empire. These mud-forts were either under the direct rule of the king or were held privately by the *zamindars* or officers of the state. The Jats, who flocked and gathered around these *garhies,* gave a tough fight to royal troops and became the veins of the great empire that arose at that time.

Some of the garhies (mud forts) were Sogar, Awar, Kasot, Sonkh, Pingora, Sewar, Dahara, Chakora, Undera, Bachhamadi, Chiksana, Ratanpur, Bhatawali, Aring, Kasot, Pingora, Jharoti, Raises, Raja Khera, Rorah, Sasni, Tuksan, Sarsoda etc.[20]

## The Bharatpur Fort

The fort of Bharatpur is unparalled amongst the forts built on plains. This fort was among the most formidable forts in India; also known as Iron Fort it is still the focal point of Bharatpur. The fort takes its name (Lohagarh-Iron Fort) from its supposedly impregnable defences. Its indigenious design gave it an awesome reputation. On account of its indigeneous style of protective and offensive aspects and queer design it is unique in itself throughout Rajasthan. It was because of this fort that the Bharatpur State became the first state in India to sign a treaty of 'Permanent Equal Friendship' with the East India Company.

The fort is situated at the distance of 32 miles from Agra, 22 miles from Mathura and 115 miles from Delhi and Jaipur. It is situated in the north-east of Banganga and Ruparel rivers on raised ravine ground. The south-western part slopes towards the fort make a low lying water-logged area around the fort. The fort orients to Agra and Mathura, the two important points of entry to Rajasthan. Perhaps,

---

18. *Tazhirah-i-Imad-ul-Mulk*, pp. 243-45 quoted by Ganda Singh; *Durrani* pp. 181-83 and by G.C. Dwivedi, *The Jats*, p. 189.
19. *Siyar*, IV, 28.
20. *J. Records*, Sarkar's coll. (Per.Ms) IX, 42, 356 and 330 (Hindi letter); VII, 337 Sitamau coll. I; 9; Qanungo, '*Bishan Singh*', proc. I.H.C. XI, 172, Quoted by G.C. Dwedi, *The Jats : Their Role in the Mughal Empire*, p. 5; For mud-forts also see G.C. Dwivedi, pp. 45-47, 114.

the fort was constructed to control these entry points and it acted as a strong guard against the passage to Rajasthan. The historians call it as the eastern gate of Rajasthan.

The fort being situated in the area of collecting waters of two rivers, the shape of the surrounding land is saucerlike or bowl like. This physical feature and surrounding forest growth perhaps attracted the Prince Suraj Mal to have a bowl-shaped fort having allignment with the ground. The moat round the fort is an evidence that water logging area easily supplied the required water to the moat and made accessibility difficult from all sides. A bowl-shaped fort was easier to defend and brought into contact, and communicated with, the various parts of the fort easily at the time of attack or emergency than the elongated or rectangular shape of the fort.

In the first decade of the eighteenth century Thakur Khem Karan Sogaria with the blessings of great saint Nagaji had built the fortress 'Fatehgarhi' on the big mound in the north-east of the State.[21] At that time the place was only a small mud fort without any formidable fortifications. Badan Singh could not tolerate the powerful partisan of Churaman in his very neighbourhood so he ordered Prince Suraj Mal to capture the fort which he did gallantly in 1733. Sogharians accepted the suzernity of Raja Badan Singh who treated them with love and affection. Realising the importance of forts as pride, prestige symbol of power and the drawbacks of weaker fort and to keep pressure on the weakening Mughal empire as well as adjacent states of Rajasthan, Raja Suraj Mal wanted to construct a very strong and invincible fort at the site.

## Fort

Folklore has it that after capturing Fatehgarhi of Khem Karan Sogharia, Suraj Mal one evening rode into the nearby jungles. There he came to a lake where he saw a lion and cow drinking water standing at no distance from each other. Naturally, so unusual a sight made a deep impression on him. In the vicinity was the retreat of a naga saint. The surroundings were idylic. Suraj Mal proceeded to the retreat and paid his respect to the mahatma who blessed him and advised him to build his capital at that site.[22]

21. Jaipur Abhilekhagar, *Jai Singh Ke naam Sahiram ka patra*, 21 July, 1419; Irvin, Vol. I, p. 414.
22. U.N. Sharma, *Jaton Ka Navin Itihas*, I, p. 193, 325-30.

Work on the fort started in January 1743. The court astrologers chose the right day and auspicious hour. Hundreds of Brahmins were fed, the blessings of Sri Giriraj Maharaj at Govardhan was sought. The *puja* took almost a week. The construction continued for a period of almost twenty years but the principal fortifications were completed in a span of eight years i.e. 1743-1750.[23]

The entire region surrounding the location of the fort is a low lying land, capacity of which to absorb water is very little, consequently, in the rainy season it becomes a marshy land. It is covered with dense forests. In the nearby hills, black and white sandstone availability in abundance, has facilitated the construction of palaces with solid stone structure. As the soil has greater percentage of clay and is marked for its binding power its mass taken out of ditch could be properly utilized for making the mud wall providing a second or inner defence line. Moat wall is made of pieces of black stones, thus forming an outer or first line of defence of the fort.

With the decline of the Mughal Empire a large number of craftsmen, masons, sculptures, and labourers were thrown out of employment, therefore, in search of the means of livelihood, they migrated from Delhi to Agra to nearby princely states where they were engaged in the construction work. The combination of Hindu-Muslim architecture of Bharatpur fort and palaces is the outcome of their dedicated workmanship.[24]

Land of Bharatpur region is noted for its fecundity and productivity on account of which the state had a rich source of revenues. The labour was so cheap that tens of thousands of masons, labourers and craftsmen could be employed to carry out the stupendous and giant task of constructing inviolate fortified gigantic structure which in the subsequent days and flight of the time was popularly known as 'Lohagarh'.

A poetic description of the forts is given in '*Sujan-Vilas*' written by Suraj Mal's court poet, Somnath. One thousand bullock carts, 200 horse carriages, 1,500 camel carts and 500 mules were employed to carry marble from Bansi Paharpur and redstone from Baretha to Bharatpur.

---

23. Ibid., p. 327.
24. Natwar Singh, *Maharaja Suraj Mal*, p. 41.

The fort stands at an altitude of 204.21 meters from the sea level and surrounds a space of 2.4 kms. in diameter.[25] Its construction is guarded by two huge mud walls one around the other. These walls are intervened by 15.24 meters deep and 45.72 to 60.96 meters broad moat. Another deep gorge provides necessary defence to the inner stone work of the fort. The moats were filled with water of the *Sujan Ganga* canal which got its water supply from the nearby *Kohini Bund*. It was always kept filled with water in which ferocious aquatics were tamed in order to ward off the enemy onslaught.

Climate of this area is sub-tropical, monsoonal, harsh and hot. Saline and oily contents of water renders it unfit for drinking. Therefore, the moat round the fort serves two fold purpose i.e., protection of the fort and softening of water in the well of its proximity. The sub-tropical climate of the region makes summers hot. In order to annul the effect of sultry summer walls of the building have been raised quite high to make the ceiling at greater heights. Proper arrangements for cross ventilation is also one of the important features of the buildings.[26]

As the fort stands in open it was very easy to break a simple line of defence in the plains because of the easy approach. This necessiated the king Suraj Mal to prepare a threefold line of defence. The city and the fort were protected in such a way that the cannon shell could not damage either of the two. If the cannon volleyed its shell straight it directly hit the mud wall without causing any damage. If it fired at even a slightly higher angle the shell making a trajectory fell beyond the mud wall surrounding the city. The inner most wall surrounding or encircling the fort is very solid. This further strengthens the defence of the fort making it invincible and inaccessible to the enemy.

The moat has two overbridges leading to the entrance gates of the fort. The gateway across the moat has massive rounded bastions and flat portals on which are painted huge war elephants in full battle regalia. One of the gates is in the north while the other makes the south entrance. The entrance on the north is over an ancient stone bridge with pointed arches and through the *Ashtdhatu Gate*. This gate of eight metals which possibly belonged to the Sisodia Rajputs of Chittorgarh, but was removed to Delhi by Ala-ud-din Khilji

25. K.K. Sehgal, *Rajasthan District Gazetteer, Bharatpur : Jaipur, Directorate of District Gazetteer, Government of Rajasthan*, 1971, p. 478.
26. K.K. Sehgal, *Rajasthan District Gazetteer, Bharatpur*, pp. 16-17.

and with the Southern gate more often called as the *Loha Darwaza,* was brought from Delhi by Maharaja Jawahar Singh in 1764. These spiked metal covered gates further add to the defence of the fort and make strong fortification therein.

The main gate of the fort is imposingly built and is of a remarkable rigidity and strength. Both sides of the gate have huge massive towers standing nearly 18.18 to 24.38 meters high connected by a portal. The side towers and the gates are intervened with two half towers of the same height. The types of towers and the gates are crowned with parapet having embrasures. The towers are inaccessively high and steep due to which chances of esclading are reduced to naught.

Furthermore, the fort has eight bastions mounted with huge guns one of which is made up of stout brass measures 4.67 meters in length. The muzzle of this cannon is 1.82 meters wide and the breach has a diameter of 2.95 meters.[27] The fort has eight bastions namely (1) *Jawahar Burj* (2) *Khan Douran Khan* or *Lala Wala Burj* (3) *Jeth Malwali Burj* (4) *Bagarwali Burj* (5) *Nawal Burj* (6) *Bhainsa Wali Burj* (7) *Gokul Ram Risaldar Burj* and (8) *Kalka Burj*. The Central tower known as the *Jawahar Burj* was raised in commemoration of the victory of Jawahar Singh on the city of Delhi in 1765 A.D. The coronation ceremony of the Bharatpur rulers which took place in this burj is regarded auspicious.[28] Nearby is an iron pillar about 12 inches (30 cm) in diameter with the names of the rulers from the time of Lord Krishna to the present inscribed on it in Hindi. The other tower, known as *Fateh Burj*, was built to remind the fort's inhabitants of the successful defence of Bharatpur from the British attack in 1805.

The town of Bharatpur then had a strong defence. It was surrounded by a wide moat and mud wall circumscribing in 11.2 kms. and having a outer ditch went into a building a 25 feet high and 30 feet broad wall which completely encircled the town. Ten big gates regulated the entry and exit namely (1) *Mathura Gate* (2) *Atal Band Gate* (3) *Bir Narayan Gate* (4) *Kumher Gate* (5) *Govardhan Gate* (6) *Jaghina Gate* (7) *Neemda Gate* (8) *Anar Gate* (9) *Chand Pol*

---

27. J.N. Creighton, *The narrative of the Seize and Capture of Bharatpur*, 1830, London.
28. R.L. Mishra, *The Forts of Rajasthan* printed by popular printers, Jaipur, published by Kutir Prakashan Mandawa (Jhun Jhunu), Rajasthan.

*Gate* (10) *Suraj Pol Gate*. These gates are fitted with long spikes. Near the gates were made a number of bastions. These gates are even used today, although the mud wall has been breached in many places and hideous unauthorised structures disfigure it.

From the point of view of safety and security the residential buildings and palaces in the Bharatpur fort are situated in the centre. The barracks of soldiers are built by the side of the boundary wall on all sides of the fort so that soldiers could immediately repulse the enemy attacks and protect the fort without giving any chance to the enemies entry. As a matter of fact, the enemy was unable to touch even the outer walls of the fort because the city itself was fortified by a thick mud wall and a sufficiently deep and wide moat filled with water.

There are three noteworthy palaces in the centre of the fort which like many throughout Rajasthan built by many generations adopted Rajput and Mughal styles but in simplified forms reflecting the Jat lack of ostentation. These are *Kishori Mahal*, *Mahal Khas*, *Laxmi Rani Mahal* and a few other residential buildings. The palaces are spacious and double storeyed and the roof are bow-shaped with elegant balconies representing Mughal architecture. The two palaces namely *Kishori Mahal* and *Laxmi Rani Palace* face eastward while one namely, *Patiyala Rani Palace* or Khas Mahal, faces northward.

Palaces of administrative importance are *Durbar-e-Khas* and *Durbar-e-Am*. The Kamra Palace to the west have a big durbar hall of historically interest. A part of this is now with the museum but it previously housed the Bharatpur state armoury and treasury. It is situated in *Chaman Bagichi* in the north of *Laxmi Rani Palace*. This was the venue of all important durbars during the princely regime of Bharatpur. Rare pieces of architecture magnify the glory of '*Kamra Khas*' which has also been embellished with numerous items and articles of beauty imported from foreign countries.

The fort of Bharatpur has within its precincts the temple of Lord Krishna under the different names, such as, *Gopalji*, *ManMohanji*, *Chaturbhuj*, *Dauji* and *Raghunathji* constructed in simple style. Similarly *Hanuman temple* are also numerous. Bharatpur fort being in the Braj region has the influence of Lord Krishna than of any other deity. This is the significant feature of the fort. No other fort has temples dedicated to Lord Krishna.

The defence of the fort was so strong that it rendered all the enemy incursions futile not to speak of scaling the wall. The top of the towers and gate is crowned with parapet and embrasures. The towers being very high perpendicular and steep provide no opportunity for escalading while any attempt from sides crossing the moat full of water and deadly fierced aquatics would prove fatal.

The fort was well protected by triple defence system in which the mud wall was an important factor, hence, it was not possible to blast the wall by mining.

Another crucial requirement of a fort was a regular supply of water to ensure self-sufficiency during a long siege. The fort of Bharatpur fulfilled this norm with equal respect of its impregnability. For maintaining potable water supply more than twenty wells were constructed inside the fort. Some of these wells were made along the side of gorge surrounding the fort. Bullocks were used to draw water from wells to supply it to the palaces and royal retinue. These wells were kept under the tight security and constant vigil in the forts.[29]

During the regime of Raja Badan Singh the capital of Bharatpur state was Deeg. His son, Suraj Mal used to run the administration and exercise his power from the capital whereas some courtiers and feudal lords used to live in the Bharatpur Fort. There are ostensible relics of sepoy barracks inside the fort all along the boundary wall. On both the sides of the road leading to *Chaman Bagichi* there was a row of barracks and stable for cavalry.

During Suraj Mal's reign treasury must have been inside the Deeg fort but subsequently with the shifting of the capital to Bharatpur, during the regime of Baldeo Singh, a *toshakhana* (treasury) was built to the south-west of '*Kamra Khas*' in *Chaman Bagichi*. This was in the centre of the fort and well guarded.

No remains of secret paths during emergency resulting from the protracted seige laid by the enemy army are found inside the fort.

Inside the fort was a provision of armoury of dimension 30.48 x 30.48 meters and 7.62 meters high located to the south-west of king's stable and in front of it is a high verandah of about 7.62 meters in height. At present a distillery is being run by the Rajasthan Government in this building. For storing the ammunition a depot

29. V.D. Sharma, *Types of Forts in Rajasthan and their Strategic Importance: A Study of military Geography, unpublished thesis*, p. 92.

was made to the south-west of the temple Mohanji. It was the best place from the point of view of safety.[30]

Historical records reveal that Maharaja Suraj Mal maintained an army consisting of well trained cavalary of 1,500 soldiers and 100 elephants.[31] His weaponary had 300 guns of different types, muskets and a lot of ammunition. Overall, the offensive and striking power of the Bharatpur fort very well vied with that of his contemporary rulers in India.

The Bharatpur fort stands on the conjuncture of many routes. Although the district was swampy tract of land covered with dense forests it was enroute from Agra to Surat during the Mughal emperor Akbar's regime.[32] The routes from Agra to Gujarat passed through Bharatpur.

The fort was unique in India from the point of view of durability, toughness and inaccessibility. However, the fort suffered from many limitations. The area of the fort being approximately 60 acres there was shortage of accommodation for men and space for storage of food stuffs. During the days of protracted seige the supply of essential commodities was disrupted and the ruler could not afford to fight for a long time.

The fort presents a conspicious specimen of a plain fort which from a strategic and defensive point of view is of immense importance. It is so well guarded and strongly protected on all sides that it has assumed the proportion of being an invincible, impregnable and inviolable fort as the enemy army was completely incapacitated to make any dent into the defence of the fort, hence it got the name of Lohagarh.

Despite the four successive attacks and long drawn seize of the fort by the British army it could not be captured.[33] The attack of General Lord Lake in 1805 was well defied by the moat surrounding the walls of the fort. Lord Lake admits that the moat was so deep and wide that his army could not cross it.[34] Maharaja Ranjit Singh harassed

30. V.D. Sharma, *Types of Forts in Rajasthan and their Strategic Importance: A Study of military Geography, unpublished thesis*, p. 93.
31. K. Natwar Singh, *Maharaja Suraj Mal*, New Delhi, Radha Krishna Prakashan, 1985, p. 141.
32. K.K. Sehgal, *Rajasthan District Gazetteer, Bharatpur : Jaipur directorate of District Gazetter*, Government of Rajasthan, 1971, p. 230.
33. Sunder Lal, *Bharat mein Angrezee Rajya* : Allahabad, Onkar press, 1938, pp. 780-87.
34. "..........I am sorry to add that the ditch was found so broad and deep that every attempt to pass it proved unsuccessful and the party was obliged to return to the trenches without effecting their object". General Lake wrote to Marquess Wellesley on 10th January 1805.
    : *The narrative of seize and capture of Bharatpur* by J.N. Creighton, published, 1830, London.

the forces of Lord Lake so much so that he had to remove the military encirclement of the fort and retreat after suffering heavy casualties. The British general could be successful only, by weaning away some perfidious commanders of Jaswant Rao Holkars army and spreading a rumour engineered by some hired astrologers who augured that an alligator would come across the seven seas to attack Bharatpur town and the fort.[35]

During the first attack on Bharatpur by the British army, the moral of the defenders was boosted by the talk of the people that Lord Krishna himself in his '*Chaturbhuj*' form has been seen defending the fort.[36] This talk of the town not only encouraged the defenders of Bharatpur but also demolarised the mercenary Indian soldiers of the British army. It was because of this fort that treaty on equal terms was signed between Maharaja Ranjeet Singh and Lord Lake on 10th April 1805.

Another onslaught of British army was faced by the Bharatpur fort in 1826 but the conditions and situation was entirely different. Rao Durjal Sal who was the regent and the uncle of the infant ruler, Balwant Singh, illegally occupied the throne. This time the Britishers were on the assault to help Balwant Singh the rightful heir of throne, to obtain his legal right. Though the fort was then in possession of illegal king but the might and strength of the fort remained the same. On 5th December 1826 Lord Combermere led his troops to attack the fort from north-east side. The attack extended from *Jangina Gate* in the north to the Mathura Gate in the east. A mine was dug on 6th January 1827 to break the wall but the explosion damaged the British garrisson and General Combermere narrowly escaped. The fort was surrendered to British forces only after a month's long sieze and that too when most of the soldiers were on the side of Balwant Singh and wished the success of British army to provide justice.

The fear of the Bharatpur Fort and the prestige shattered off the British army could easily be sum-up by the letter which Sir Metcalf had written to the Governor-General about the feeling prevalent in general public and among his own men. The days are gone when people took to their heels even at the sight of white face and red

35. R.L. Mishra, *The Forts of Rajasthan*, Jaipur, Popular Printers, 1985, p. 61.
36. Sunder Lal, *Bharat Mein Angrazee Rajya* : Allahabad, Onkar Press, 1938, p. 794.

i. Baradari over Museum at Bharatpur (Facing Page 48)

ii. Lakshman Mandir in the market of Bharatpur (Facing Page 48)

iii. Kishori Mahal in the Bharatpur Fort (Facing Page 48 Back)

iv. A View of Deeg Fort (Facing Page 48 Back)

garment. The great part of military prestige of the British lay buried under the unfortunate sieze of Bharatpur fort.

Before the arrival of aircraft the Bharatpur fort was almost impregnable. The most formidable fort in Hindustan combined Hindu Mughal architecture which fascinates and merits the attention of modern architects for the studies of its subtleness and specificity.

## The Fort at Deeg

To the east of the Rupsagar, one can see the massive citadel of Deeg built by Suraj Mal at the command of his father Badan Singh.[37]

Badan Singh on the advice of a holy man Pritam Das[38] decided to make Deeg his capital. A strong fort was needed at the capital for security and protection. With this view he ordered his son to built a strong fort there. Suraj Mal intended to built the fort on the top of a pahartal, a mile westward to the town of Deeg, but on Jai Singh's intervention[39] he had to drop the idea and construct it on a level plain.[40]

The formidable castle of Deeg is nearly square in plan. With one large round bastion at each corner and two smaller ones on each side, the area approximately measures 300 sq. m. If the outer defence of the fort is excluded the space enclosed is about 274 m. square.

The massive masonary walls made of rubble and mud towers, up to 85 feet (28 m), are exactly oriented along the cardinal points as the Rup Sagar, Badan Singh's palace and all the other buildings at Deeg.[41]

These walls are strengthened by twelve imposing bastions, four on the corners and two on each of the four sides, and, entered by a single door or breach in the wall on the north. The curtain, which is also square, has two more bastions and the gate facing the west. The largest and the most imposing bastion is '*Lalka Burj*' on the north-western corner and the '*Hazara Burj*' on the south-eastern corner. Lalka Burj is still mounted with huge and rudely wrought iron guns of small calibre. There is a moat around the fort which is 50 feet

37. Baldev Singh, *Tarikh-i-Bharatpur*, Ms. pp. 27-28, cited by Ram Pande, *Bharatpur*, p. 34.
38. K. Natwar Singh, *Maharaja Suraj Mal*, p. 22.
39. Baldev Singh, *Tarikh-i-Bharatpur*, Ms. pp. 27-28.
40. U.N. Sharma, *Jaton Ka Navin Itihas*, I, p. 326.
41. J.A. Devenish, *The Bhawans or Garden Palaces of Dig*, p. 49.

(17m) broad. This shallow ditch is filled with water.

The walls are coated externally with plaster which has peeled off at many places. The lofty rampart varies in height at different places. It appears that the building has not been completed and it was intended to raise the ground within the fort to the level of the lower part of the rampart as it has been partly done in the south by filling it up with earth to that level and then to erect the whole rampart to an equal height.

The only entrance is on the northern side by a bridge over the moat connected with the only gate. As the thick masonry of the inner curtain has been cut through to give access to the interior it is evident that this entrance and bridge were added afterwards, and by examining the wall of the northern front near the abutment of the bridge, it may be noticed that the bridge formerly led directly into the castle instead of through the outwork.[42]

Like Lohagarh, the Deeg Fort has a threefold line of defence. Inside the walls are the remains of an inner earth work. A part of it looks over the high outer walls. It was utilized for the fortification and a big gun was mounted on top. This strengthened the defence of the fort making it inaccessible and invincible to the invaders.

The capital Deeg had a strong defence which furthermore, added to the impregnability of the fort. The huge mud wall encircling the town of Deeg is about 7.24 km in circuit. This wall was so prodigious in height and breath that it appeared at the first sight "like a long range of hillocks utilised for the purpose of enclosing the city."[43]

There are ten gates in the fortifying wall i.e. Au, Bandha, Bhura, Dilli, Govardhan, Jasondi, Kama, Panhori, Ramchela and Shahpur gates. The wall between the Panhori and Shahpur gates is in masonry but the rest of it is of mud.

A broad and deep ditch runs all around the city except near the Shahpur which commanded the main entrance. Shahpur was almost a fortress by itself with "an area of fifty yards square on the inside for the use of the garrison and presenting four commanding bastions facing the four cardinal points,.....About a mile from this place, and nearly in the centre of the town, which is strongly built.....the ramparts are high and thick, furnished with masonry."[44]

42. J.A. Devenish, *The Bhawans or Garden Palaces of Dig*, p. 49.

43. *Le Nabob Rene Madec* : Sec. 48, quoted by Qanungo, *History of the Jats*, p. 165.

44. Major William Thorn, *Memoirs of war in India*, p. 414.

The approaches to the outer fort were rendered extremely difficult by a number of fortified outworks and small *garhies* scattered all over the surrounding plain. The strongest and the largest among them was Gopalgarh, a small garhi which stood at a short distance opposite the Shahpur.[45] Now the mud wall of the fortification is dilapidated and hideous unauthorised structure disfigure it. Beside the masonry bastion in the fort there are two more bastions in the interior, one in the north-east and other in the south-west, the former of which is called Dhruvtila. It is even higher than the Lalka Burj.

There are few noteworthy palaces in the fort. Like the Lohagarh the residential palace is in the centre of the fort. It is built in the centre for security and safety. Probably this palace, which belongs to Badan Singh was constructed sometime before the outer walls of the fort were constructed.[46] This palace is constructed on an elevated ground. The plan is conventional. All the roofs of its upper and lower stories have fallen and the only servicable part of it that remains are two barracks in its exterior compound sometimes used as the jail.

The architecture of the palace is attractive and striking. The employment of red sandstone and the use of pointed arch in the construction is noteworthy. The balconies and carved window gratings above the fine doorway are all dilapidated.

Behind the palace on the east is a '*chhattri*' of Sultan Singh, the younger brother of Raja Suraj Mal. This was kept clean and worshipped daily.[47] And adjoining it is the Muslim tomb believed to be that of Mirza Shafi, Mir-Bakshi in the Delhi Court. He was killed near Au on the 3rd September 1783. To the east and south-east of these cenotaphs are two extensive grain stores capable of containing vast quantity of stores of every kind.

The defence of the fort was so strong that it splitted the sudden attack of the enemy. It was futile to speak of scaling the walls. In reconnoitering the defences of the fort the heart of Mirza Nazaf Khan filled with suspicion at the closer view of its strength. So numerous were the guns and matchlockmen manning its wall that the fort appeared to him a 'living valcano', every inch of which seemed

45. *Le Nabob Rene Medec* : Sec. 47, quoted by K.R. Qanungo, *History of the Jats*, p. 166.
46. J.A. Devenish, *The Bhawans or Garden Palaces of Dig*, p. 50.
47. Jawala Sahai, *Dig, its history and palaces*, p. 19.

to emit fire and send forth an inexhaustible flood of molten lead. The fortifications were so extensive that his whole army was considered hardly sufficient to blockade effectively even one side of it.[48]

The fort of Deeg fulfilled the crucial requirement of regular water supply during a long siege. For maintaing the regular water supply in the fort there are more than thirty wells both in the rampart and in the fort. These wells were kept under the tight security and constant vigil in the fort. In order to supply the water to the palaces bullocks were used. Few of these wells were dug along the side of the gorge surrounding the fort.

The fort of Deeg in one way is more durable than the Lohagarh Fort. It has godowns for storage of food stuff. During the days of siege the supply of essential commodities must have been regular and there must have remained ample fodder for the animals.

The view from one of the bastions of the fort displays the outer ramparts of the city. The hills that now divide the Bharatpur State from Gurgaon and Alwar can be seen on the north and west horizons; to the east is the road to Govardhan and Mathura, to the south stretches a low-lying plain across which may be discerned the road leading to Kumher and Bharatpur and the bund that held up the lake on the border of which the famous battle of Deeg was won. To the west, close under the walls of the fort, are the *bhawans* and gardens laid out by Suraj Mal.[49]

Though humilated by the neglect for more than one and a half century and overpowered by enemies, the fort still keeps erect the Lalka Burj lifting its head high into the sky. The strength of it makes it almost inaccessible to the enemy especially in the rainy season.

## Fort at Kumher

Kumher is a village situated at a distance of about 16 km. from Bharatpur and about 18 km from Deeg. The village has an area of 14.2 sq.km. It is surrounded by a mud wall built by Suraj Mal.

Kumher is the third in importance after Bharatpur and Deeg as seat of Jat government because of a strong fort built by Suraj Mal

48. K.R. Qanungo, *History of the Jats*, p. 167.
49. J.A. Devenish, *The Bhawans or Garden Palaces of Dig*, p. 51.

in the reign of his father Raja Badan Singh. It is important because it lies midway between Bharatpur and Deeg and the army based here could assist both the places at the time of need.

Kumher was earlier known as Kuberpur. The place is said to have taken its name from its founder Kumbha, a Jat of the village Sinsini, about 10 km. to north-west.

Unlike the forts at Bharatpur and Deeg this fort is not surrounded by a ditch. But like Bharatpur and Deeg there is another rampart probably the city wall, surrounding at a distance of "two or three kos" followed by *marhala* at a distance of one kos. The wall of Kumher was literally lined up with cannons atop. All this had rendered this fort quite impregnable.[50]

The main gate is in the eastern direction. It is built up of red sandstone with natural arch. Entering the gate are two chambers on opposite sides with semicircular roof still printed of yellow colour. On the western side is also a gate from which a flight of stairs lead to the entrance.

The fort is presently in a ruinous state. It is painful to see such a strong castle turned down in such a dilapidated condition. Nothing is left in proper order except few rooms at the first floor that too ccupied by the villagers.

This fort has five storeys. The walls of the fort are quite high to heighten the ceiling of the fort, which is properly cross ventilated. The fort is located near the main road and realising it Suraj Mal built a *parkota* to strengthen its defence. By using such tactic the cannon shell could not damage the walls of the fort. Such arrangements for the protection of the fort made it almost inaccessible. The Maratha batteries failed to make any impression upon the walls of Kumher and their main army was held at bay by the resolute Suraj Mal.[51]

Unlike the fort of Bharatpur it has no bastion but the unbroken ramparts (totally ruined) had bastions to protect the fort. Like in the Lohagarh and Deeg Forts the palace and the residential places are situated in the centre. All around were barracks for the soldiers who could immediately defy the enemy attacks to protect the fort.

50. *TAL.*, 215; Wendel, *Memoirs on the Jat Power, pp. 49-51, Siyar*, IV, pp. 27-28; *Sujan*, p. 222; *TAH.* 1096; *Majma-ul-Akhbar, in Elliot* VIII, p. 361, quoted by G.C. Dwivedi, *The Jats*, p. 115.

51. Qanungo, *History of the Jats*, p. 52.

There are places of interest in the fort though in a ruined state. It includes a harem palace built by Raja Badan Singh. The gate of this palace has multifoliated arch. It was probably on the third floor. A narrow gallery, screened with obliquely cut jalis, runs at the back of the above floor. There is a big hall at the back of which is a long corridor with plain floor and bow shaped cells at each end.

The palace of Rani Kishori is another place of interest in the fort. After the death of Suraj Mal she started living in Kumher.[52] Now in a dilapidated condition this palace would have been glittering at her time.

Inside the palace she built a temple dedicated to Kishori Shyam ji.[53] At the centre of it is Tulsi Gamla connected with a corridor and four gateways at either side. Paintings of cows, lions, two holy men pouring water can still be seen in the fort.

The defence of the fort was designed in a manner to provide no opportunity for escalading. Najaf Khan, who conquered Deeg after a stiff resistance from Ranjit Singh, could not conquer the Kumher fort untill and unless the Jat raja escaped from it. It was in such situation that the enemy for the first time scaled the walls of the fort since it was built.[54] The walls of the fort was no doubt built very high, perpendicular and steep, providing not even the rarest chance for escladíng it.

The fort was unique not only in Jat region but in India from the point of view of inaccessibility not as much because of its toughness and durability but because of its strategical importance.

52. *Patrika*, Shiksha Vibhag Bharatpur Dwara Prakashit Tatha 'Jagriti' Printing press Dwara Mudrit, p. 30
53. *Ibid*., p. 30.
54. *Ibratnama* Ms. p. 346.

Kumher, besides being midway between Bharatpur and Deeg, was situated in the centre of a great "sandy plain with no spring of fresh water."[55]

In selecting the site Suraj Mal obviously wished to keep himself free to fall from behind on either side in case the enemies, considering their greater importance, concentrated on Deeg and Bharatpur. And if in view of his presence here enemy converged on Kumher there remained the scope for harassing the enemies on both sides from Bharatpur and Deeg while the enemy's encampment on a sandy and waterless plain would have fully exposed them to the fort artillery as also to nature's fury in the hot months.

The provision stocked in Kumher fort were in such abundance that no other fort in India could rival it. Its formidable ramparts were literally lined up with small and big pieces of artillery. A few long range heavy cannons placed atop were such as would not permit enemy to come any where near the walls.

Though the area of the fort was not very large but it was so well-built that there was no shortage of accommodation for men and space for storage of food stuffs. During the days of protracted siege the supply of essential commodities was undisrupted and the ruler could afford to fight for a long time.[56]

With masterly defensive strategy Maharaja Suraj Mal succeeded in thwarting the designs of a formidable combination of 80,000 men. This fetched him and his fort "high reputation" all over India.

Though the fort presents a conspicious specimen of inaccessibility it suffered from many limitations. The first and foremost amongst them was the regular and fresh supply of fresh water.

It was because of the richness of its land in producing salt that it got the name Kuber (God of richness) which later on became Kumher.

The water in the wells was all blackish and it was only from the tanks or wells at long distances that good drinking water was procured.[57] Though scarcity of fresh water was a boon against the besiegers it was also a curse for the besieged.

55. Wendel, *Memoirs on the Jat Power*, pp. 49, 122.
56. Kumher contained provisions sufficient to last "more than a year" during the Maratha siege between Jan.1754–May1754; Wendel, *Memoirs*, pp. 49-50, 122.
57. Munshi Jwala Sahai, *Dig, its history and palaces*, p. 17.

## Fort at Wair

Raja Badan Singh in the centre of Bhusawar, Bayana and Ucchain established a new *pargana* Wair and left it in the possession of his second son, Pratap Singh.

The Wair Fort was constructed under the supervision of Pratap Singh. In 1726 A.D. an ancient hillock was surrounded and a massive strong hold was constructed on top of it. The entrance to the fort is from eastern and western sides. The gates of the fort are huge and strong, which have iron sheets and big iron nails. It has *marhala* in order to protect these gateways.

A *kuccha parkota* was constructed around the fort with a cirumference of about two kms. There was a shallow but broad moat around this parkota which has now dried up. To fill the moat of the fort a canal was constructed which is known as Sita Nahar and a dam named Sita. To enter the city were five *pakka* doorways. In the north towards Bharatpur and Kumher, in the east towards Bayana, in the south towards Sita, in the west towards Bhusabar[58], of all two still exists.

The walls of the fort were externally coated with plaster which has peeled off at many places. These walls are strengthened by imposing bastions, five on the corners and two each on every side. They could be scaled by the stairs running up to the exterior wall. Like the Lohagarh and Deeg Fort, the fort at Wair has a threefold line of defence. Remains of inner earthwork can be seen near the wall which was utilized for the fortification. A gun mounted on top of the bastion is still existing. It made the fort invincible and inaccessible to the invaders and thus strengthened the defence of the fort. The wall was also enormous in length and breath.

Entering through the eastern gate one finds the palace of Pratap Singh. Peeping through its balcony one could see the *Phulbari* and *Safed Mahal*. The architecture of the palace is attractive and striking. The fort itself is surrounded by palaces, *kachari*, *barood khana*, armoury, soldiers residence and well for water supply. Armaments and explosives manufactured here were supplied regularly to the Jat kingdom.[59]

---

58. Sudan, *Sujan Charitra*, p. 247.
59. *Modave* (ms) p. 184.

In the vicinity of the fort were beautiful gardens and palaces. On account of the abundance of trees it was once called *Naulakha Bagh* and another garden with the palace *Safed Mahal* in it is called *Phulbari*.[60] Poet Somnath has beautifully described the fort, palaces and gardens in his verses—

वेर की शोभा निराली है।
चतुर्दिक वृक्ष, गुल्म, अनेकों बाग, सरोवर विद्यमान हैं।
चतुवर्ण के शूरवीर यहां निवास करते हैं।
बुलंद महल तथा गढ़ सौन्दर्य सुषमा के प्रतीक हैं।[61]

Raja Bahadur Singh (son of Raja Pratap Singh) who held the fief of Wair refused to acknowledge the authority of Jawahar Singh after Suraj Mal's death and decided to declare himself independent. So this fort unfortunately faced the onslaught of his own kinsman. This assault was made in August 1765.[62] The fort proved very powerful and even after a siege of three months Raja Jawahar Singh was unable to capture it by force. By treachery and false peace proposals it came under the Bharatpur rule once again. But the fort like other Jat forts proved its invincibility.

## Fort at Aring

Aring is a large agricultural village lying at the centre of *Tehsil* of Mathura. It is situated in 27°29'N and 77°32'E, at a distance of twelve miles from headquarters on the metalled road from Mathura to Deeg. It is generally accounted as one of the 24 *Upbans*.

There are ruins of a mud fort built during the last century by one Phunda Ram, a Jat, who held a large tract of territory in '*jagir*' under Suraj Mal. Suraj Mal attacked and demolished the *garhi* of Thakur Khema Jat of Fatehpur who was a partisan of Churaman but could not be killed. Suraj Mal ordered Phunda Ram to complete the expedition. Phunda Ram ultimately killed him (c. 1753).[63]

This fort is now in a dilapidated state. It is double stroyed and it is built on a higher plain and at a place of strategical importance.

---

60. The marble swing in front of the Gopal Bhawan was removed from this place and placed at Deeg during the third quarter of the nineteenth century.
61. Somnath, *Peeush Nidhi*, chapya 23.
62. K.R. Qanungo, *History of the Jats*, p. 105.
63. *Tawarikh-i-Hunud*, 20b-21b; quoted by Dwivedi, *The Jats*, p. 100; also see Ganga Singh, *Bharatpur ka Itihas*, I, p. 136.

The fort has vaulted roof built up of *Lakhori* bricks. It has a hall whose roof has totally fallen. The staircase is completely broken and one cannot climb to the first floor. There are three chambers on the right side of the entrance. They are double storeyed and at places baked bricks are also used.

There are three arched doorways which are strategically important. There are open windows on the west so that a vigilant eye may be kept on the enemy's movement and the passerby.

A tringnometrical survey station lies in the fort at an elevation of 670.5 feet above the level of sea. The upper markstone of the survey station is on the vaulted roof of the old fort and is about 57 feet above the level of the surrounding country.

It was one of the strong castles netted all around the Bharatpur kingdom and was an important vein of the empire.

## Fort at Thun

The fort at Thun is situated at a distance of eleven miles to the west of the Deeg. This formidable fort was built by Churaman II in a low marshy and thickly wooded tract.

Churaman II became the undisputed leader of the Jats in 1695. During the period between 1688-1695 a large number of Jat *garhies* had been occupied or demolished by the imperialists. Churaman built this new fort in the impenetrable forests for the purposes of defence and preservation of booty. To construct it he was aided by the hidden wealth of his ancestors including Raja Ram.[64]

According to Shivdas, "Thun was surrounded by so thick a jungle of thorny bushes that even the birds found it difficult to pass through it. Its rampart was as high as 'heaven,' while the moat around was so deep that water burst up from the bottom."[65] The chief defence of this fort was a belt of impenetrable forest.

Sawai Jai Singh accompanied by Raja Gaj Singh Narwari, Maharao Budh Singh Hada of Bundi and Maharao Bhim Singh Hada of Kota took command against Churaman and besieged the fort of Thun. The fort of Thun with its lofty ramparts, a very deep ditch and thickly - wooded environs was rendered fairly strong. Churaman was said to have gathered grain, salt, ghee, tobacco, cloth and firewood

64. Wendel, *Memoirs on the Jat Power*, p. 16.
65. Shiv Das, *Shah Nama Munawwar Kalam*, p. 19; *Iqbal Nama*, p. 23 (both Askaritrans).

for twenty years. The prudent Jat had turned out empty-handed all merchants and traders - before the siege began. He assured the traders of compensation if he emerged victorious.[66]

This siege from (November 1716–April 1718) proved of no use. Jai Singh was harassed firstly by the surprise attack of the Jats and secondly he had to steer his way through the impregnable and thorny forests to Thun to invest it effectively.

After the death of Churaman the second expedition of Sawai Jai Singh to subjugate Thun was ultimately successful. In this expendition he was aided by Badan Singh, the nephew of Churaman II.

Jai Singh began by cutting down the jungles to breach the unpenetrable fort. It was not the might of Jai Singh's army but it was the treachery on the part of Badan Singh which guided him to the vulnerable spots in the defences of the fort of Thun.

Maukham Singh, son of Churaman, gallantly defended Thun for two months (October-November, 1722). He escaped from the fort with darkness of night. Jai Singh in the height of glory was impatient to enter the fort and fall a victim to the Jat stratagem. Badan Singh who was convinced by Maukham Singh's treachery, dissuaded the Raja from going inside the fort and prevented a major disaster. Hardly had Jai Singh decided otherwise when the fort mines began to explode "hurling the stone through the sky." This incident proved the wisdom of his foresight for which Jai Singh was highly thankful to Badan Singh. Attempts were made to trace out Churaman's treasure but all in vain. The city and fort of Thun were demolished and the soil was ploughed by asses by Jai Singh to make it detestable in public eyes. The fort thus being upset is since then called '*Ondha Thun*.'[67]

66. *Shiv Das*, pp. 19-20; *Iqbal*, pp. 26-27; Irvine, *Later Mughals*, Vol. I, p. 324; Qanungo, *History of the Jats*, p. 31; Dwivedi, *The Jats*, p. 68.
67. *Tawarik-i-Hunud*, 17a-18b; *Majma-ul-Akhbar*, Elliot, Vol. VIII, p. 361; Thun was, however, rebuilt, though on a different site, well before Wendels arrival in the Jat country. *Tawarikh-i-Hunud* (19b) relates an interesting incident that during the Maratha invasion of Bharatpur (1754) Malhar Rao, in order to assuage Maukham Singh ploughed the site of the former Thun with elephants and sowed pearls. G.C. Dwivedi, *The Jats*, p. 91.

## Fort at Sonkh

Situated 10 kms. (6.25 miles) from Govardhan and 16 miles south-west from Mathura and 18 miles south-east of Sinsini the fort of Sonkh of Khutel clan of Jats lies in 27°31' E. Nothing but some crumbling walls and bastions remain of this old fort. This fort at present is in the possession of Archaeological Survey of India. At present, it is a protected monument and excavation is being done to go deep into the study of the mud hillock of this historical fort.

The first reference of this castle goes back to September 1688 when Bedar Bakht and Bishan Singh laid siege to Sonkh which was on the way to Sinsini from Mathura. The imperialists defeated the Jats who assembled to defend the castle. The fort finally fell after the siege of four months, September to December in 1688.

There is another *garhi* by the name Sonkh Gujar 10 miles to the north-west of Bhatavali in the Kathumar area. This newly built garhi by Churaman was the venue of struggle between Hari Singh and the Jats led by Fateh Singh and Churaman. This fort was captured by Hari Singh, the Rajput general on 9th January, 1693 after a fierce fight.[68]

## Badan Garhi

This is situated at a distance of about 5 miles from Bayana. Now this place of historical importance is totally ruined. Having fled from Sinsini the family of Braj Raj sought refuge in this small and obscure mud fort. Here, one of the wives of Bhao Singh gave birth to a posthumus son named Badan Singh. It is after the name of this personage that the garhi is still known as Badan Garhi.[69]

## Fort at Jwara

It is situated 2 miles to north-east of Mursan. It was built by Nand Ram Jat who surrounded it with a network of small *garhies*, the prominent among them were Kihrari and Jagsana. Hari Singh, the general of Bishan Singh, lost his life in attempt to capture it on

---

68. K.R. Qanungo, *History of the House of Diggi*, see for these two *garhies*, pp. 65-66, 87-88 respectively.
69. 'Odier Settlement Report, Bharatpur', referred to by Ganga Singh, '*Yadu Vansh*', pp. 47-48, Somnath, '*Dirgha Nagar Varnan* (Kashi Nagri PraCharini, Hindi Ms) p. 3, '*Ras Peeushnidhi*'' and '*Madhav Vinod*' in Somnath Granthawali (ed. by Sudhakar Pande, Kashi, 1971 AD.) pp. 3, 318.

v. Bridge on the Moat of Ramgarh Fort (Facing Page 60)

vi. Gate, Parkota, moat and its bridge-Ramgarh Fort (Facing Page 60)

vii. Armoury in Ramgarh Fort (Facing Page 60 Back)

viii. Building in Ramgarh Fort (Facing Page 60 Back)

5th April 1695. It was one among the many castles which gave stiff resistance to the imperialists. At present only a heap of mound is seen which do not even reflect the glorious past of this *garhi*.[70]

## Laher

(Etah 27°53' N, 78°41 E) - To the west of the village the remains of a '*garhi*' (now heaps of mound) is discernible with vestiges of towers. The garhi probably erected in mud was 50 m long, 40m wide and 6 m high beside the course of old Ganga. It is said that this garhi also faced the same fate of devastation in 1857 revolution by English men. The local chieftain a Jat was killed in the encounter and the citadel was raged to ground. A mound on the south of the citadel spreads in 100 x 60m in area and with 2m high.

## Ramgarh at Koil

Sabit Khan, Governor of Koil region during the time of Farrukh-Siyar and Muhammad Shah built a fort three miles north of the town Koil and named it Sabitgarh. After the occupation of the Koil by Surajmal in Februaury 1753 from its *faujdar* Rao Bahadur Singh Burgujar, the fort was renamed Ramgarh. Surajmal and Jawar Singh made Ramgarh a stronghold of the Jats. According to News Letter dated 11th June 1761, Surajmal was staying in Ramgarh. Mirza Najaf Khan captured Ramgarh from Jats in 1775 and named it Aligarh. In 1804, the Britishers named Koil region also as a separate district called Aligarh.[71]

Though smaller Fort it is surrounded by rampart and moat. The gate facing south-west and bridge on moat are still intact. Inside the fort, wells and armoury are in ruinous conditions. With the efforts of former Union Minister Nurul Hassan, the fort was given to Aligarh Muslim University for Botanical Garden (Fort).

70. Qanungo, *History of the House of Diggi*, pp. 110-115.
71. J.M. Siddiqui, *Aligarh District : A Historical Survey*, pp. 25-27, 112; Sudan, *Sujan Charitra*, pp. 98-103, *Tarikh-i-Ahmad Shahi*, p. 47a.

1. Main Gate (Kumher Fort)

2. Palace of Rani Kishori in dilapidated state (Kumher Fort)

3. Interior view of Kumher Fort

4. Steep and perpendicular outer wall (Kumher Fort)

5. Sloping path probably used by the horse riders which runs to the second storey (Kumher Fort)

6. Shish Mahal (Right), Badan Singh's Harem (Left) (Kumher Fort)

7. Sloping path running down from Jawahir Burj in the rear is Kishori Mahal (Bharatpur Fort)

8. Outer Wall (Kumher Fort)

9. Asht dhatu gate (Bharatpur Fort)

10. Fort at Sonkh

11. Chronology of Bharatpur rulers,
Iron pillar Jawahir Burj (Bharatpur Fort)

12. Another view (Fort at Sonkh)

13. Entrance (Fort at Aring)

14. Trignometrical Survey Station (Fort at Aring)

## *Chapter 5*

# Palaces and Mansions

The palace architecture of the Jat rulers of Bharatpur may broadly be divided into two groups. The first group consists of the garden palaces of Deeg. The beauty of this architecture is the beauty of presentation and treatment. The palaces are developed logically. Formality, balance and symmetry are the important part of this architecture. The peculiar feature of these palaces are marked by sophistication, regularity based on an order, and profuse and delicate carvings besides their double roof, emphasized on the exterior by lower and upper eaves.

The material used for the construction of these palaces is stone, brick and mortar, and the edifices are either faced with sandstone, slabs of pinkish colour or finely plastered. The exceptions being the marble and red sandstone encasement used at Suraj Bhawan and the palace inside the fort. The variety of material used largely for these palaces is somewhat harder and better suited for sculptural work, though not very inviting to look at.

The architecture is primarily of trabeate order. The general features of this architecture are hypostylar halls, engrailed arches resting on ornate pillars, flat roof-terraces, balconies and pavilions with Bengal roofs, double eaves, moderate structural heights and spacious internal arrangements. Projecting dripstones, pillars with floral bases and tapering shafts normally surmounted by capitals bearing carved flower petals are other attractions of Jat style. Though the palaces do not bear imposing character but each of them possesses delicacy and dignity. These palaces are entirely of secular order.

The second group consists of high class houses known as 'havelis', 'mahals' which are becoming fewer and obsolete. These mansions are seldom found except in towns and large villages, and are generally two storeyed 'dumanjila'. They are built around '*Chowks*' (quadrangle or central plot or yard) with stone or fire-baked brick walls, tile roofs and verandahs.

Entry into them is through a gateway or passage in one of the outer walls of the buildings. From the inner court a few steps lead to the verandah or 'chaupar'. In the verandah, it seems that strangers were received, children or women sat or talked.

The ground floor generally has four to seven rooms, a central hall, a back verandah and the second storey has four rooms or two halls. In some places such types of houses have two open squares surrounded by rooms and verandahs. The first where the men live, and the back one set apart for women. A privy is attached to a distant corner either in the front or at the back of the building according to convenience. There may be a rear yard with flowers and trees and a 'tulsi gamla' in a masonry pillar pot.

From the architectural point of view these mansions, with a few exceptions have little beauty or ornamentation; even the finest are plain, massive and monotonous.

The ceilings are made of small, closely fitted 'thiris'. The pillars generally rise from a carved stone. The roofs are either terraced or covered with flat tiles. The staircase are in the walls, sometimes narrow and dark.

I have selected palaces and mansions of Deeg, Bharatpur, and Vrindaban which exhibits both categories of architecture rspectively. Besides the above mentioned mansions there are hundreds of palaces belonging to the second group scattered in every nook and corner of the Braj region and till Delhi and Shimla. Some other striking palaces include mansions at Agra, Kamar, Mathura, Sahar, Bharatpur, Wair and Barsana.

## Palaces at Deeg

The bhawans or palaces of Deeg are built on a perfectly leveled plain with a central ornamental garden, along edges of a vast oblong path guarded by two grand reservoir on the east and west. The cornerstone of this whole structural group is the fourfold design of the central garden. The principal edifices are situated just above the outer end of the four garden canals. From this place the whole plan of the garden and the grouping of the buildings around it are easily discernible.

To locate all the buildings in their order it is necessary to walk round the terraced sides of the garden. Starting from the Gopal

Bhawan flanked by the Bhadon Bhawan on the right, the first building facing northwards along the southern side of the square is Suraj Bhawan. At its back, on the opposite side looking into a separate quadrangle, is the Hardeo Bhawan. On the same side of the square, next to Suraj Bhawan, is a small arched verandah or arcade, the narrow space between it and the Suraj Bhawan being formed into a sheltered recess. Further downwards is the wall of the immensely elevated tank in which the water supply for the fountains is stored.

The next building is the Kishan Bhawan in the centre of the terrace facing north. At its back is a large courtyard. At the corner of a garden the picturesque curved roofs of the old palace of Badan Singh may be seen with their spiked bunch of foliage standing out against the skyline. The front entrance of Badan Singh's palace is at the far end. Moving along the eastern edge of the square, the great masonry reservoir Rup Sagar comes into view.

The Keshav Bhawan looks over and adorns Rup Sagar, looking from it eastwards over the water the huge walls of the Deeg Fort dominate the view. With the triple domed and corbelled window overlooking the water, on the opposite side at the corner, is the graceful building Shish Mahal. Moving along the edge of the garden, past the vinery and then turning the corner is the Nand Bhawan occupying the centre of the broad terrace of the northern side of the square. This was intended originally to form the central feature of an even more magnificant scheme of architecture than was accomplished.

The building of three other pavilions was commenced to enclose another square garden. One of these, the Ram Bhawan was nearly complete, another Chander Bhawan was left half built, and of the third, to complete the square, only the foundations are to be found. The intermediate space between these unfinished buildings has been blocked by walls and the public road crosses it so that this part of the scheme is hidden. Passing the Nand Bhawan and again turning the corner the terrace of the Gopal Bhawan is reached with the Sawan Pavilion on its left thus completing the circuit. The principal entrance to the enclosures is now through the Singh Pol situated opposite the Suraj Bhawan on the north; the two remaining gates, though modern, are the Nanga and Suraj Gates built almost on the south-western and north-eastern corners of the bhawan premises respectively.

Before describing each building seperately it is necessary to throw some light on the architecture and forms of construction of the Deeg palaces. They have been built on a level plain, on raised stone, paved terraces, some six feet above the level of the garden pavements. Fergusson, speaking about these palaces says, 'They lack the massive character of the fortified palaces of other Rajput states but in grandeur and conception and beauty of detail surpass them all.[1] The style and methods of construction are as distinctly representative of Hindu art as the buildings of Fatehpur Sikri are of Mohammadon although in both places features have been adopted from either style.[2] The architecture is simple yet inviting and it presents a welcome variety of aspect when compared with the severe conventional outlines of Mohammadan art.[3]

The form of construction depends on the materials, massive blocks and slabs of sandstone. Sandstone was quarried in required sizes and shapes according to the power of transport and were split to any desired thickness and length. Immense slabs were laid flat over projecting cornices to form the roof and also the overhanging slender drip-stones, and the stone-panelled facades and walks. The domes, the towers and the lofty arches of Mohammadan art have been avoided, and there is consequently an impression of greater stability.[4] According to Fergusson, the roof system of the palaces contains stone except the central part which, after being contracted by a bold cove, is roofed with a flat ceiling. This seems to have been considered a defect because nothing but stone has been used in other parts of the palace.[5]

The use of arcuate system has been made at some places though the architecture is primarily of trabeate order. Mostly the arcades are of a decorative quality as each arch is formed by joining two spandrel shaped slab cantilevers projecting from the pillars.[6] Though the form of arch is copied from the Mohammadan style there is not a single true arch in the palace and the openings have been virtually covered by two brackets meeting in the centre. The arcades of these buildings may be characterised as more elegant than rich.[7] The other

1. James Fergusson, *The History of Indian and Eastern Architecture*, p. 178.
2. J.A. Devenish, *The Bhawan or Garden Palaces of Dig*, p. 20.
3. *Ibid.*, p. 20.
4. *Ibid.*, p. 20.
5. James Fergusson, *The History of Indian and Eastern Architecture*, p. 179.
6. M.C. Joshi, *Dig*, published by the Director General Archaeological Survey of India New Delhi, p. 8.
7. James Fergusson, *The History of Indian and Eastern Architecture*, p. 179.

general feature of trabeate order is hypostylar halls, engrailed arches resting on pillars, pavilions and balconies, moderate structural height and spacious internal arrangements. Amongst other varieties of arches, the limited use of semi-circular trefoil and pointed apses too is worthy of note. The pointed type of arch of the Jat architecture is not a copy of Tudor arch of the Mughals but resembles its certain earlier types with a sharply-pointed apex and rounder curves.[8] The glory of Deeg consists in the cornices which are generally double, a pecularity not seen elsewhere and which extent of shadow and richness of detail surpass any similar ornaments in India, either in ancient or in modern buildings.[9] The lower cornice is the usual sloping entablature, almost universal in such buildings. The upper cornice, which was horizontal, is peculiar to Deeg and seems to have been designed to furnish an extension of the flat roof which in eastern palaces is usually considered the best apartment of the house.[10] The designers have successfully combined the system of the earlier water-palaces with the scheme of a formal Mughal garden. Nowhere a single mansion stands very prominent and none of the principal palaces appear to be subordinate to each other. It appears that the Jat architects have perhaps symbolized the relatively democratic set-up of their own village-community. This is also reflected in the dietary setting where no table was laid and every one sat on the floor to dine together. Politically too the Jat ruler of Bharatpur was primes interperes, a peer among equals.

The framework of the buildings was such that the lintels, pillars, bedstones, cornices, brackets have their places and dimensions assigned to them by cannons of art and architecture hereditarily transmitted to the descendant. For each separate stone in an arcade there is a name and a method of fixing known to craftsman. The general design of each edifice was probably sketched to scale and chisell for record on a convenient slab of stone.[11] The building then proceeded according to rule, the patterns of the carving being sketched out on the stone themselves as they were being shaped at the site of the work. Fergusson thinks that the greatest defect of these palaces is the style, while they were being erected was loosing the true form of lithic propriety. The form of its pillars and their

8. M.C. Joshi, *Dig*, published by the D.G.A.S.I., New Delhi, p. 9.
9. James Fergusson, *The History of Indian and Eastern Architecture*, p. 180.
10. M.C. Joshi, *Dig*, published by D.G.A.S.I., New Delhi, p. 9.
11. J.A. Devenish, *The Bhawans or Garden Palaces of Dig*, p. 25.

ornaments were best suited for wood or metal than for stone architecture.[12] The bhawan complex at Deeg carries behind it a thought befitting a retreat based on the luxurious Mughal ideal of earthly paradise on the one hand and the romantic tradition associated with the Indian rainy season on the other.[14] Each Bhawan possesses a dignity and delicacy though not bearing a very imposing character which strengthens the harmony between architecture and gardens, not obstructing the unity of conception. The significance of these palaces are hypostylar halls, flat roof-terraces, balconies and pavilions with Bengal roofs, balanced outline, attractive and logically-disposed arcades, greenery, double eaves, charming tanks and canals with fountains - forming a confluence of beauty, comfort and grace.

## Gopal Bhawan

First and foremost in importance is the Gopal Bhawan, situated on the West of the quadrangle and facing the east. It is built entirely of grey sandstone. 'It combines the elegance of Shah Jahan's palaces with the most robust character of Rajput architecture, and being better adopted to the amenities of modern life than the earlier fortess palaces of Rajputana, it is especially interesting to the modern architect.[15]'

The central hall of it projects out from the east front. It is an arcade, the front height of which extends from the terrace to the roof. A smaller arcade of the same height projects similarly from the opposite water frontage. In each wing of the building the same height is divided into two stories. There are also two floors below the level of the terrace on the water face, the lower of which is submerged when the reservoir is full. The hall is divided lengthwise into two portions by a row of four pillars in the middle of its width. These pillars carry five arches parallel and opposite to the projecting five arched front, and the roof slabs are laid on cornices across the two rows of arches. The interior length of the front is 77 feet, the arches being all 12 feet in span. The clear width on each side of the inner row of arches is about 26 feet, the pillars at their base being 2 feet 3 inches square. Thus the full width is about 54 feet. The height from the floor to the ceiling is about 24 feet. The hall thus dimensioned is larger than the Westminster House of Commons, except in height.[16]

12. James Fergusson, *The History of Indian and Eastern Architecture*, p. 180.

14. M.C. Joshi, *Dig*, published by D.G.A.S.I., p. 9

15. Havell, E.B., *Indian Architecture*, p. 217, John Murray (1924).

16. J.A. Devenish, *Bhawans or Garden Palaces of Dig*, p. 26.

The projecting half of the hall has one arched opening each facing north and south, these openings being 15 feet in span. The back of the hall is formed by the central wall of the buildings. This wall is eight feet thick and there are domed alcoves though the thickness of it, looking outwards into the main hall and inwards into a set of rooms on a raised platform, is about seven feet above the level of the main floor. These rooms are approached by steps from the passages at the two ends of the hall. The passages are low and narrow, being built within the thickness of the walls, and the doorways leading into them are too low for modern ideas, though they may suffice for oriental needs, the narrowness of these communications exemplify how the interior architecture is designed for display rather than for accommodation.

The acloves in the wall have been treated like kiosks in miniature in their decoration, the opening pierced through the wall being decorated with the semblance of domed roofs carved in relief against the face of the wall. Their curved and pointed eaves are wonderful examples of delicate stone carving.[17] The same type of decoration is applied symmetrically to the interior surface of the room within, every ornamental part having its counterpart. The terraced roof is given more than its usual importance as a place of ride taken for pleasure in the cool evening by the omission of domes and cupolas and by being extended on all four sides beyond the walls of the building by a bracketed parapet of pierced stone work. The combination of this parapet with the usual wide dripstone beneath it, which protects the walls from rain and sun, forms the strikingly characteristic cornice of the whole building more original and beautiful in form than the useless "designed cornices of Italian Renaissance palaces, which only serve the purpose of providing constant employment for plumber plaster and paper hanger by diverting the flow of rain water from the exterior to the interior of the building."[18]

There are similar raised floors and alcoves in many well known halls of audience and it is conceivable that the chiefs may have used them occasionally to sit in state above the level of their subjects on the floor below; but certainly the design of these and other chambers was ruled by the craftsman's scheme of ornament and the uses of them were casual. A devious passage through the walls and underneath

17. Devenish, J.A., *Bhawans or Garden Palaces of Dig*, p. 27.
18. Devenish, J.A., *Bhawans or Garden Palaces of Dig*, p. 29.

the raised floor leads into a fine arcade or hall projecting from the western water-face. This has three equal arched openings in front and one at each end looking north and south respectively. The view from this hall when the doors are swung back, leaving the archways open, is picturesque: in front, the large reservoir 30 feet sheer below, a garden beyond, and at the sides in the distance an animated scene, the steps crowded usually with people washing themselves, their clothes, and their cattle at the water's edge.

Foliated Hindu arches show that Suraj Mal gave employment to the craftsmen who since the time of Aurangzeb had ceased to work at the Mughal Court. The construction of these wide openings on the bracket principles, in two blocks of stone, instead of by radiating voussairs, is usually attributed by the western critic to an obstinate Hindu prejudice against the western arch. Really it is the simplest, most practical, and most artistic way of dealing with such a form when good buildings stone of sufficient size is easily procurable.[19] The arched openings in the ends look along the facade of the bhawan with its graceful window balconies and overhanging eaves in view, flanked on either side by a domed pavilions carried by carved stone brackets projecting over the water.

Returning to the main hall one can see that on each side of its interior portion, is a double-storeyed wing. One wing is almost identically similar to the other, any slight differences being due mainly to modern alterations. The space in each storey is divided by pillars and arches to support the roof and to satisfy architectural requirements but rather awkwardly for purposes of accommodation. The upper floor is gained by the usual staircase, low, narrow, steep and dark. The upper storey looks down into the hall through arched and pillared openings. There is a dais or raised floor[20] separating the main rooms of each wing longitudinally, but as there are alcoved openings through its walls, the apartments have no privacy except by modern expedients. Eight habitable suits of rooms can, however, be found; as either wing has four storeys each storey is divided into two suites, one looking out over the garden and the other over the water.

---

19. Havell, E.B., *Indian Architecture*, p. 219.
20. *Nashewan* in Persian.

The whole of the interior walls are beautifully panelled in stone with nitches, flowers and simple geometrical devices carved there on in relief so that no space requiring decoration is left bare. Space will not permit a detailed description of all the architectural features, which do not differ greatly from those of other buildings of the same style but a few remarks may be noted at random.

The private apartments of Gopal Bhawan occupy the north east and west side of the building. The north front faces a large bathing tank and is charmingly diversified by a number of balconies and two large open pavilions with typical Bengali roofs. Placed on the side of the grand canal at Venice it would be acclaimed as the most delightful of Venetian palaces.[21] The slabs of stone forming the roof are more than 27 feet in length. The havoc that is being wrought in them by the rusting of the iron cramps can be seen from below. The iron rings fixed into the stone work inside and out for curtains and the cover of canvas used for shelter have also done much damage.

The drip stones or eaves overhang the walls eight feet. The grouping of the brackets carrying them is worthy of notice; they are grouped in clusters so as to distribute greater weight on the stronger parts of the wall thus reducing the load over the crowns of the arches. The carving of the brackets and of the soffits of the panels laid over them is worthy of admiration. That the bracket is almost exclusively an original Indian form of capital can, I think, scarcely be doubted but the system was carried much further by the Mughals, especially during the reign of Akbar, than it had over been carried by its original inventors, at least in the North. The Hindus, on receiving it back, luxuriated in its picturesque richness to an extent that astonishes every beholder; and half the effect of most of the modern buildings of India is owing to the bold projecting balconies and fanciful kiosks that diversify the otherwise plain walls.[22]

21. Havel, E.B., *Indian Architecture*, p. 219.
22. Fergusson, J., *History of Indian and Eastern Architecture*, pp. 180-81.

The lower tiers of brackets is on the same level as the inner cornice. The roof slabs laid over them inside keep them steady. Above these come the sloping drip-stones laid on a ledge supported by the brackets, above which there is another tier of brackets carrying the parapet. The thickness of the roof therefore extends from below the drip-stone to the top of the upper tier of brackets. The folded iron excrescence on the roof is obviously modern as well as two little annexes at the sides. The doors and windows are also modern but without them the building could neither be preserved nor inhabited.

The side wings of the palace seem to have been planned as purely residential suites. Of these, each comprise a front and back hall of moderate dimensions with a central corridor and rooms of different sizes on either side in both the stories. The frontage of each hall is pierced by three arched opening and on the ground floor the existence of four pillars, forming a central group and housing inside a fountain basin, catch attention. A room of the northern wing contains a throne or throne platform of black marble and another of the southern of white marble and both these are believed to be spoils of war removed by Jawahar Singh from the imperial palaces of Delhi.

Attached to the main facade of the Gopal Bhawan is a tank (10.97 by 7.62 M) having as many as fifteen fountains and flanked by two canals with jets planned along with angles of the facade. The local boys delight in jumping off from the ledges and even from the eaves into the deep reservoir.[23] The brick and plaster parapets round the terrace and reservoir are, it is almost needless to say, not of Suraj Mal's time; however, it is a matter of thankfulness that they are not worse, for the taste of the last generation inclined strongly towards corrugated iron.

The stone gateposts were erected by Maharaja Balwant Singh who carried out a great deal of useful work at Deeg without dis-figurement to the buildings. These gate-posts are favourable examples of minute superficial decoration; this being the characteristic of the later style to which Bharatpur architecture has degenerated, having lost boldness and proportion of outline.

---

23. Devenish J.A., *The Bhawan or Garden Palaces of Dig*, pp. 30-31, Calcutta (1862).

The imaginative setting and commendable architecture of Gopal Bhawan, competes well with other palaces of contemporary Rajput princes. Being a big and beautiful building its reflection in the surrounding sheets of water creates a fascinating charm in the environs.

## The *Sawan* and *Bhadon* Pavilions

The Gopal Bhawan is flanked by two detached kiosks in the north and south sides, known as Sawan (month of July-August) and Bhadon (month of August-September), the two chief rainy months of the Hindu year. Each pavilion is built on a rectangular counter fort hanging from the western face of the terrace of the bhawan on the Gopal-Sagar, they are in confirmity with the alignment of the western projection of the palace and accentuate the general architectural effect of the whole group. The lower storey consists of a hall with gallery at the back and verandahs separated by means of piers carrying the arches on three sides. The storey has its floor at the water level when the reservoir is full but for the greater part of the year the water is usually 10 feet or more lower so that the tier of brackets bearing the projecting verandah of the lower storey can be seen, and the beautiful carved struts at the outer corners where the brackets need support from below. Within this verandah overhanging the reservoir there are fountains of various kinds sprays, cascades and jets.

In the middle of back wall of the gallery is a wide carved chute, for the charming flow of water, which is connected through a hidden drain with a shallow oblong cistern in the hall and a flatish water-sprinkling basin in its centre. On the outer side of the hall, above the spandrels of the arches, copper pipes are fitted so that the water falling through them in the form of a semi circle on the verandah may play during the summer heat; the dripping days of the rainy season can be imitated in advance, so delightful in reality, when at last the clouds cool the burning air and bring greenness to vegetation of the sun-baked land.

The facades of the verandah are decorated with embowed openings having finely-carved latticed rails. At the base of the structure the brackets, supporting the verandah and particularly the long stuts of the corners, impart to it the shape of a keel which lends the whole composition the look of a large floating boat with a cabin at the top. The ground before the upper storey is worked into a garden of usual type having intersecting canals with jets for communicating the idea of the greenery caused by rains. The curved domes of the roofs with their rows of spiked bunch of foliage along with apex of the curved ridge provide an admirable contrast to the long horizontal lines of the Gopal Bhawan. The convex roofs are domes generated by segmental curves from an oblong base.

The building has five cusped arches borne on fluted pillars carrying the roof along its longer axis and three of the same size along the shorter. On the terrace facing the Gopal Bhawan there is an inlaid marble platform surrounded by a marble arch placed most effectively in the centre line of the row of fountains pointing east. The arch is gracefully proportioned to its purpose, which was to carry a swing. The platform and arch, if local information is correct, was brought from the palace at Wair and fixed in its present position by the advice of one of the first political agents at Bharatpur. Originally it may have come from Delhi.[24]

The eaves are brought to segmental arch sweeping boldly over the arched sides and from the curved based above the eaves the domed roof springs moulded roundly inwards and upwards till the opposing curves meet along the ridge which is parallel in its curve to the eaves of the longer sides. The domes may be conviniently termed ellipital.[25] The same shape of roof is used for the window balconies of the water-face of the Gopal Bhawan. The spikes may be supposed to mark the tent poles placed in a row and the corners of the pointed over hanging edge of tiles stretched by guy ropes to pegs in the ground. An ornamental pattern made of straight lines is maintained in the railings of the steps leading down from the trace to the lower storey, it gives a true impression of lightness to the pillars and arches of the verandah which have little weight to carry.

## The Suraj Bhawan

A beautiful building built of marble and named after Suraj Mal is somewhat improperly located. It consists of a single storey and is a square of 26.80 M and symmetrical in every detail with a

24. J.A. Devenish, *The Bhawan or Garden Palaces of Dig*, p. 32.
25. J.A. Devenish, *The Bhawan or Garden Palaces of Dig*, p. 32.

flat roof (above 6.70 M). The rich material and general architectural treatment of the Suraj Bhawan reminds one of Shah Jahan's architectural products and its design too bears affinities with certain earlier Mughal edifices.

The exterior was not quite finished in Suraj Mal's or Jawahar Singh's time and the eave-stones, upper tier of brackets and the parapet railing are cut from white sandstone. This part of the work was well executed by his descendant Maharaja Balwant Singh who ruled a generation ago.

The Bhawan was originally intended to carry an upper storey, the bed-stones for which are placed on roof. The marble employed herein belongs, entirely or partially, to more than one of the royal buildings of the Mughals for the slabs used in its wall do not always match in size and texture. This building is supposed to contain the marble slabs of the royal school for the princesses in the Red Fort, Delhi, which probably was one of the many victim's of Jawahar's fury. In addition to this the Jats appear to have also used some fresh marble which did not belongs to any previous edifice; this is evident from the definite stamp of Deeg-architecture on some of the constituents of Suraj Bhawan. It is possibly due to Jawahar's death that the encasement of the structure remained incomplete. The idea to cover it with white marble more probably was an afterthought for certain pavements, its plinth, major portion of the western face and a large number of eaves and brackets are still in sandstone. In order to give them the resemblance of marble, with the exception of the plinth, they have been coated with a fine variety of lime plaster.

Each face of the building has a deeply recessed *verandah*, open in front, with five eight-cusped semicircular arches extending along with middle half of the side and rooms flanking at the corners which have dome shaped ceilings decorated like many Mughal buildings with a single carved lotus. The remaining quarters of each face of the building are being enclosed by panels that indicate the position of the inside passages and the width of the verandah on the transverse faces. At each corner of the building there is a square room, the outer walls of which are each formed by a panel enclosed within a two cusped elliptical arch of the same width as the verandah. The floor of every verandah ornamented with a central tank containing jets was to serve as an object of beauty for the structure as well as for its occupants. The inner wall of the verandah is pierced by windows, the sills of them being at the level of the verandah plinth and approached by steps at either end. In the centre of the verandah in front of the fountain there is a large alcoved window, the shutters of which slide into grooves in the walls. In two niches, one on each side of the central opening, there are miniature windows and there is another window at each flank, these looking out from a passage that gives access to the rooms within.

The central room of this palace has a flat roof laid over the cornices of the walls. At its side is an oblong chamber about 22 feet x 9 feet. The vaulted ceiling of this chamber is formed by three elliptical domes supported and divided by arches. At each corner there is a chamber 9 feet 4 inches having a fluted dome for its ceiling springing from a circular cornice. These chambers are all connected with each other by doorway openings.

The groins of the domes of the square chambers are decorated with lotus buds at their points. The panelling is treated with the utmost grace of line and the vivid shapes of the niches pierced through the walls specially excite admiration. The dados of the central apartment, the marble floors of the corridors and cells around are bordered with excellent pietra dura work. The curved ceiling of the corridors supported by semi circular arches are worth looking. Several slabs contains plants executed in pietra dura by Mughal lapidories. The flowering plants represented are bolder in size than any one to be seen at Delhi or Agra though the stones used are perhaps not so minutely inlaid or so precious.[26]

The marble floors of the rooms are all inlaid with geometrical patterns. Those in the alcoves are inlaid in a network pattern in lapis-lazuli. The stones principally used are lapis-lazuli for blue, blood stone for green and jasper for deep red cornelian, mother-of-pearl, malachite, yellow stealite and agates are sparingly used. The lime stones provide diversely coloured tints of brown and yellow for the floors and of the lower portion of the wall unfortunately during the last decade of 19th century the inlaying has been very much damaged but still it reflects the utmost beauty of its past.

The internal arrangements of the Suraj Bhawan are more like a pavilion than a place of residence and this was probably designed

26. J.A. Devenish, *The Bhawans or Garden Palaces at Dig*, p. 37.

for the exclusive use of ladies as a place of rest and recreation. The sandstone structure with a verandah and side compartments on the east of Suraj Bhawan has perhaps been erected to preserve its architectural effect. Flanked by tanks and garden on the sides and aided by the features of Deeg architecture this building in the marble clothing, no doubt, is graceful.

## The Hardev Bhawan

To the south, behind the Suraj Bhawan, lies this royal ladies dwelling forming a charming quadrangle around an attached inner garden. It is kept private by high screen walls, built by Maharaja Suraj Mal, along two sides of the quadrangle to block the view of it from the roofs of the other bhawans. A set up of this kind was very common with royal abodes of the middle ages in India especially of the Mughals. This palace does not appear to be an original part of the main bhawan complex considering its situation at a corner. Most likely this was later on rebuilt by Suraj Mal to suit his taste and requirements. Possibly its northern wings were demolished to accommodate the Suraj Bhawan. A closer examination of the structure itself supports this assumption; however, the back portion of the building seems to be original.

The entrance to the enclosed quadrangle is between the eastern side of the Suraj Bhawan and a small arcade built close opposite to it so as to form a sheltered recess between the two verandahs adorned by fountains and trees; this recessed passage is always shaded, as it is open only on the north, and it is one of the most picturesque parts of the garden. The principal block on the south is double storeyed and stands in an impressive portion overlooking the accessory garden. The lower storey consists of a projecting central hall faced with arches springing from a row of double pillars. Behind the front arches is an arcaded colonnade running along with three sides of the inner group of four pillars roughly resembling those available within the side wings of the Gopal Bhawan. At the back of the hall is an oblong corridor with a raised floor and domed cells at each end, a feature also common to the Suraj Bhawan but much simpler otherwise. A rectangular chamber with a verandah flanked by cells has been built on either hand of the hall.

On the east a comfortable ramp provides access to the upper storey adorned with wooden doors and fanlights painted blue and green is no doubt comparatively modern and other parts have been constructed at different periods. This has an iron fencing central terrace and two pillard *dālāns* to its right and left. The hind part of the terrace is occupied by a crowning chhattri bearing a spiked curved roof attended by miniature side domes. This kind of grouping imparts the building an effective composition. A narrow gallery screened with obliquely cut stone *Jalis* run at the back of upper floor. In one corner there is a coach house. This has been constructed by dismantling the eaves from two adjoining old building and fixing iron girders across the intervening space. At the back of the Hardeo Bhawan, facing the public road, there are galleries protected for privacy by perforated screens.

The secluded position of the Hardeo Bhawan suggests that it was solely meant for the royal females. The other two sides of the quadrangle have ordinary rooms flanking a central verandah which is in two floors on the east. There is nothing special about the garden of the Hardeo Bhawan except that it is of a strictly private nature appropriate for ladies quarters. The jets studded in the four garden canals are very small and are modelled after the lotus bud without any sculptured body. But it is difficult to assess whether this was the original form or a later change.

## The Kishan Bhawan

On the south side of the quadrangle built of grey sandstone is the Kishan Bhawan. Rising amidst the southern fringe of the complex this pretentious fabric is a very handsome carved stone pavilion, the arcade of which is open only on the north side. It comprises a well decorated panelled facade[27] (8.84m high) broken by five large central archway and enriched by the presence of a charming tank with thirteen fountains on its terrace. Its structural grace is further increased, besides the dripstone, by three short ornamental projections of the parapeted roof.

The archways communicate with a large hall (19.20 by 16.45 m) lately used as the tehsil court,[28] akin in some respects to the main hall of the Gopal Bhawan. In the centre there is a row of cusped arches, five in number, the spandrils of middle and front arches are

---

27. The facade is beautifully panelled with niches; the variation in ornament and proportion from that of the other Bhawans being sufficient to prevent monotony.
28. J.A. Devenish, *The Bhawans or Garden Palaces of Dig*, p. 40.

adorned with thickly carved arabesques. There is an elliptical two-cusped arch in the frontage at either wing of the arcade, each of these arches being closed with panelling that contains a door (now blocked) with a very graceful carved grating over it. On the back wall the striking feature is an alcoved balcony with exuberantly carved front side. Its curved roof with delicate details representing a foliaged hut and ornate flanking members demand special attention. Sculptured peacocks and tender flower plant also embellish some of the structural accessories of the hall. The fine projecting eave-stone running along with frontage is surmounted by a parapet wall and perforated railing without the upper tier of brackets. The railing at the top projects out, however, in the platforms from which guns are fired, one rectangular, at the centre on brackets, and a semi-octagonal, one at either flank corbelled out. These barbettes break up the flatness of the parapet most efffectively. Along each shorter sides of the hall are two rooms at the back a long corridor with raised floor which leads to a small cell with a half decagonal plan projecting from the southern wall. Inside the arcade it will be found that there is the usual dais at the back but the building can be more easily seen than described. It is rather a pity that the closed room in it are used only for lumber. If these were cleared out and the doorways in them opened a better view of the architecture would be obtained.[29]

The southern part of the flat roof of the Kishan Bhawan is surrounded by a pretty arcaded pavilion called *Solah-dari* or sixteen doored pavilion, that is to say, it has five arches on the long sides and three transversely at either end accentuating the vertical effect of the fabric. The pavilion has the prevailing double tier of brackets the upper ones above the drip-stone carrying the parapet. The double tier of projections to finish a roof is called a *raj-ros*.[30] This pavilion was added afterwards by Raja Balwant Singh (1826-1853). From its position on the roof it looks down into a large courtyard where elephants fight and similar entertainments were held.

## The Nand Bhawan

On the north of the quadrangle is a magnificant edifice raised on the terrace. It is the Nand Bhawan, rectangular in shape with an area of about 45m by 26m. It comprises an extensive oblong hall or

29. J.A. Devenish, *The Bhawans or Garden Palaces of Dig*, pp. 40-41.
30. *Ibid.*, p. 41.

arcade measuring 66 by 40 feet built of grey sandstone resembling an auditorium occupying the grater part of the block. It is enclosed by a grand arcade of seven openings and narrow walled wings on the longer and shorter sides respectively. The eastern and western ends of the building are enclosed by panelled walls, pierced by windows looking out from a raised floor covered by intercommunicating compartments. The walls are decorated with ornamental alcoved balconies, three of which facing the hall are in marble inlaid with semi-precious stones. Similar decoration also occur on the large sunken basins of marble fixed on the floor of hall between the shorter sides of the central arcade and side wings. It is quiet likely that the material used in balconies and basins came from Delhi as part of the booty.

The curved eaves shading the window openings project from the semblances of segmental domes carved in relief on the panelling. Overhanging the walls on every side there are wonderful sloping eaves carried on richly carved brackets, the drip-stones being decorated at their edge with a hanging ornamented curtain rod of bedstead. Above the drip-stone there is a tier of brackets surmounted by a shelf, fringed in the same manner as the eaves. The railing or parapet that should be above this flat ledge has never been constructed because the building was not quite finished when the 'debacle' occured otherwise there might have been an upper storey and the ugly staircase covers on the roof would not then have been necessary.

The ceiling of the central portion of the hall was formerly roofed with sal beams supported partly by an inner group of pillars and arches arranged in a rectangle and partly by the facades each containing a row of seven arches borne by fluted pillars. These seven arches are not similar, the middle five of them being semi-circular and ten-cusped, while the terminal ones are of larger span and therefore elliptical and two-cusped according to the usual variation. The arched openings have been filled with glass doors in order to preserve the building and make it habitable and so the great hall is now enclosed on all four sides instead of being open north and south. The rectangle within the inner pillars measures 67' x 40' leaving 21' to be spanned at each side and at each end of the inner group of pillars. The span of the arches being about 11', there are two rows of five arches in the inner oblong running parallel and opposite to the middle five arches of the facade and three arches transversely at the shorter sides.

The roof between the two inner rows of pillars 40' wide was formerly supported by wooden sal beams, the lower sides of which were carved and the intervening space between the beams were filled with sal planks carved in the same manner, the whole forming a handsome wooden ceiling. On the top of these beams were brick pillars 2.5' high and these were connected with stone slabs supported on ordinary terraced roof. This structure being excessively weighty and it was noticed for many years that the roof had sunk considerably in the centre and that several of the beams had been much decayed. This inner portion of the roof however collapsed during the reign of Raja Balwant Singh. In 1866 Lieutenant Fredrick Home R.E., the state executive engineer replaced the beams with seven wrought-iron-girders procured from Roorke workshop and fixing tie rods connected them with brick arches on which the ordinary flat roof laid. The carved ceiling consisting of 3 inches *sal* planks being attached to the lower flanges of the girders, the appearance of the room remained unchanged while the roof has been indestructible.[31]

The terracing of the flat roof is five feet in thickness, hollowed out in tunnels for lightness whenever the *durbar* may wish to effect the renewal of the Nand Bhawan roof- a very expensive and difficult undertaking- the props and girders will serve as the necessary scaffolding and they can afterwards be removed. The two wings of the building contain chambers on a floor raised about eight feet above the floor of the main hall into which they look through alcoves decorated with the similitude of domed kiosks in the same manner as the miniature domes indicate. The marble is richly inlaid, but it will be observed that the inlaying was never completed, the decoration having evidently been stopped while it was in progress.[32]

In front of the vaulted recess at either end of the hall extending across, there is a beautiful marble fountain cistern or bath about 40' x 20' sunk a little below the level of the floor, the bed of it inlaid with a network pattern in black marble. Beneath the vaulted recess there is a lower storey, the floor of it being a little below the level of the bed of the fountain. These bhawans were formerly open with the means of accommodation and protection, Maharaja Jaswant Singh improved them by applying ornamental shutters adjusted in wooden

---

31. Munshi Jwala Sahai, *Dig its history and Palaces*, Printed at the tribune press, Lahore, 1902.
32. J.A. Devenish, *The Bhawans or Garden Palaces at Dig*, p. 47.

frames to all their large doors and windows and providing them with abundant English furniture of every kind.

## The Keshav Bhawan

On the east side of the quadrangle is a pleasantly situated square pavilion commanding the view of Rup Sagar Tank on the one hand and the Keshav Bhawan more commonly known as Baradari on the other. This Bhawan occupies a remarkable position of the artificial lake amid the western section of its ghat, a portion of which seems to have been utilized for constructing this large structure by the designers. This is an open square building with double verandas on all sides and triple line of fountains on the edges is placed on a platform having projecting semi-octagonal external angles recalling the pattern of the bases of corner-minarets or towers of Mughal structure.

Each of its faces is composed of five noble arches serving as vertical passages for light in gracing it externally. A glance at the ornamentation of the arches will show that the building was put together before the carving- which is always done on the stone lying flat on the ground - was quite completed in some places. It looks that the builders were impatient of delay.[33] The beauty of the building lies in its fanciful internal arrangements, some of which were aimed to create a sensational scene of the rainy season. The bhawan is diversified centrally by an arcade running on all side and forming an inner square which is separated from outer one by means of a 0.91m wide canal encircling it. The canal is bordered on both of its edges by tiny jets and has a bolder row of large fountains in the middle.

Although not stressed outwardly as the other buildings the mansion bears a double roof which was utilized once for featuring entirely strange items, that is, the artifical thunder of clouds. This devise was operated with the pressure of water passing to the lower roof through certain hollow pillars of the structure with considerable force and thereby rotating some heavy lithic balls kept on it which created the internal sound. The water, when released from the roof through the pipes above the arches, set an exhibition of rains and the fountains, while in full play during a sunny day, completed the imagination by producing a rainbow.

---

33. J.A. Devenish, *The Bhawans or Garden Palaces at Dig*, p. 44.

## The Shish Mahal

The Shish Mahal (Glass palace) standing very close to the Purana Mahal was built by Nawal Singh, a son of Suraj Mal. Now a dilapidated mansion it looks very picturesque from outside but the interior is very disappointing, the courtyard being full of rubbish. At present only its hind part is in the original state with crowning 'chhattris'. Due to the proximity of Rup Sagar it has pleasant sight. Except certain ruined round arches and pillars, there is nothing of architectural merit except the "hammams" or Turkish baths on one side of the courtyard which are also dilapidated; possibly because of their decorated character involving the use of glass the edifice got its present name. It would be a good work to clear the rubbish and to restore it.

## Badan Singh's Palace

To the south of the Rup Sagar stands the palace called the Badan Singh's mahal or Purana Mahal. There is only a narrow passage (now blocked) between the Kishan Bhawan and the north wall of Badan Singh's Mahal. Built by Badan Singh, it had a robust and stately exterior. It was planned as a spacious rectangle with an interior composed of two separate courts engirded on all sides by ranges of compartments, vestibules and chambers. Although less refined in character, architecturally it is more sound than the bhawans.[34]

The palace has two floors but at certain places it wears three storeyed blocks to emphasize the structural effect. It is massively built in a different style i.e. without the expensive ornamentation of the bhawans. Entering from the fine and old doorway there is a covered passage which does not lead directly into the quardangle but takes a little turn to one side of the doorway. The lightning of the passage is obtained from narrow openings pierced high up through the massive outer wall and splayed inwards, thus giving the impression of a possible need of defence from an outside attack.

Some importance can be attached to certain obliterated wall paintings inside the gate leading from the eastern court to the inner one. The entrance chamber seems to have been painted by the painters of Mughal and Rajput Schools. The paintings consists of popular

---

34. M.C. Joshi, *Dig*, New Delhi 1971, p. 30.

decorative designs on the ceiling and scenes depicting episodes mainly from the life of Krishna and figures of a few Brahmanical deities, besides elephants and horses. All these are executed on the stucco plaster sticking to the wall which itself serves as the background. The painted figures have a restricted and simple colour scheme, bold outlines and angular manipulation tending to roundness in the form of flowing garments.[35] The depictions are flat and the scenes suffer from lack of perspective. In the treatment of the trees the painter seems to have followed the pre-Mughal schools of western India. However, there appears to be some Mughal impact in the dress and structures delineated there.[36]

The building which is arranged by the side of two square quadrangle, one leading into the other through another gateway and guarded the passage. The first courtyard or *mardana* is utilized at present for the tehsil court and treasury by the state government. The inner court has been considerably altered. It was for the safe keeping of Badan Singh's numerous queens where they must have somewhat crowded although there is a large range of chambers built in these stories.[37] Both the quadrangles are surrounded by high walls but the side of the *zanana* quadrangle facing Rup Sagar has an elegant project balcony from the wall supported on brackets and carrying a row of *jharokhas* or domed porches as coronating components is no doubt remarkable.

There are pair of pavilions with curved tartar roofs, one on each side of the quadrangles, each having a row of nine long spikes pointing upwards from the bow-shaped ridge and as their ridges are at right angles to those of the gate way domes, the view in perspective of the group is very striking.

## Mansions at Vrindavan

At Vrindavan, near Kesi Ghat, are the two handsome mansions built by Rani Kishori, the senior Rani of Maharaja Suraj Mal and Rani Laxmi wife of Randhir Singh. In both the palaces the arrangement

---

35. M.C. Joshi, *Dig*, New Delhi, 1971, p. 30.
36. *Ibid.*, p. 30.
37. J.A. Devenish, *The Bhawans or Garden Palaces of Dig*, p. 43.

is identical with that of a medieval college carried out on a miniature scale but with extreme elaboration of detail. Both the buildings are disposed in the form of a quadrangle with an enriched gateway (in the case of Rani Kishori's mansion it is all broken and lying in a dilapidated condition) in the centre and opposite is a temple of more imposing elevation than the ordinary domestic apartments which constitute the two flanks of a square.

## Rani Laxmi's Kunj

It is a mansion of high architectural merit. The entrance is from the north. On entering through a verandah a square courtyard can be seen. On the left of the courtyard is a temple dedicated to Laxmi Mohan. The temple front of Rani Laxmi's Kunj (such being the distinctive name for a building of this character) is a very rich and graceful composition. It has a colonnade of five arches thoroughly naturalized standing on a high plinth which, like every part of the wall surface, is covered with the most delicate carving and is shaded above by unusually broad eaves which have a wavy pattern on their under surface and are supported on bold brackets. On the right, arches and collanade are identical but on a lower plinth, beautifully carved and full of architectural merit. The structure is five storeyed but appears to be three storeyed building from the entrance. The first storey can be seen from the side of River jamuna on the bank of which this mansion stands; on the second storey is the temple of Kesi Mardan (the Kesi Ghat got its name from the Kesi Mardan); on the third storey lies the main structure and the beautifully designed temple; on the fourth storey is the choburja (two in all, both in east and west). At the centre of the courtyard is 'tulsi gamla' built on approximately a foot high plinth and is presently in a partly destroyed state because of a pipal tree growing in the courtyard. The other tree growing in the courtyard is 'mor chhari'. Three gates of the mansion open in the north towards the Jamuna (the ghat) and two in the opposite direction in east and west.

It is said that the present Raja of Bharatpur has sold this beautiful mansion which was once a pride for the royal family to some Chaturvedi as it appears from the sign board right on top of the entrance of this historic monument.[38] At present the keeper of this elegantly carved, and once the dreamy rest house of Suraj Mal's

38. Told by a resident to the researcher.

consort, is Shri Mohan Lal Sharma who is the Head Master of the primary school. From the Bharatpur State he used to receive Rs. 130 per month in which he has to pay the electric charges. The Government should preserve this graceful mansion which has been praised in the past by the foreigners and which still adorns like a gem in the midst of Braj Bhoomi.

## Rani Kishori Kunj

This mansion now in a dilapidated condition, is of much plainer character in nature. It is a square and a high enclosure beside the river Yamuna. It is built up of red stones which are beautifully carved. The enriched gateway is now all broken. Carving on redstone is seldom seen in the buildings of Bharatpur royal house. On the left and right of the courtyard are three thoroughly naturalized arched verandah. The engraving on the walls is very elegant and beautiful with flowers and petals. Now this palace is occupied by families (mostly Bengalis) which have settled down in Vrindaban. The whole structure is composed of three stories, two for residence and one beside the ghat. On the south of river Yamuna along the course of water is a balcony with three windows, all opening towards the river. The verandah attached to this balcony is *kacha*. There are four rooms, two on the either side of the verandah, and a flight of steps lead to the other comparatively small cubicle attached to the balcony which have a window opening towards the river. The Rani used to sit in the balcony for a view to the river. After bathing she may be using the cubicle as a change room. But by now the river Yamuna has changed its course and it flows at a distance of about a furlong from the balcony. The scene of the river from the balcony is still very picturesque.

At the right side of the entrance, on a plinth about three meters in height, is a temple constructed by her and dedicated to Kishori Mohan. (For the details of this temple, See Chapter VIII.)

## Badan Singh Kunj

Near Kesi Ghat is situated Badan Singh's Kunj looking less impressive in comparison to the other two magnificant Kunjs of Rani Laxmi and Rani Kishori. This was built by Thakur Badan Singh, though large it has no architectural merit.

The Kunj is a *Dumanjila* (two storeyed). This is built around a chowk (quadrangle); it is built on a very high platform (the reason may be that this palace is situated near the river). The flight of steps lead to the main gate (At present the stairs are broken and it is a bit difficult to reach the gate) which is built of red stone. Entering through the gate is an enclosure having three arched entrance which leads to a verandah. May be it was used to receive strangers. It is built up of lakhori (*kakiya*) bricks. Inside it, is a dalan or courtyard. At the end of the courtyard, on a plinth with the similar three arched verandah, is a chamber which probably was a temple. At present a family is residing in the chamber. The palace has seven rooms in all.

There is a rear yard with flowers and trees and a holy basil in a masonry pillar pot of the two open squares surrounded by rooms and verandahs, the first may be used by the male while the back one set apart might be used by the women.

On the left and right side of the inner verandah are two tibaris which have a door each and three arches now closed by bricks. On both sides of the courtyard are the staircase which are narrow and lead to second floor. This floor also has a courtyard with rooms on either side. Each room has three doors. From the roof of this kunj, Khapatia Kunj, Laxmi Kunj, Rani Kishori Kunj can be seen. Behind it is attached the Bedi Kunj.

From the architectural point of view this palace has little beauty or ornamentation. Though it is monotonus and massive yet it is plain in character. The roof is covered with plain tiles. Badan Singh may have constructed this kunj to stay whenever he came to Vrindaban for religious pilgrimage.

## Ganga Mohan Kunj

The most striking palace at Vrindaban is the Ganga Mohan Kunj built by Ganga, the wife of Maharaja Suraj Mal.[39] The building has a high and massive basement storey. The entrance gate has a natural arch built of cream coloured stone which is elegantly carved. On the either side of the wall is the figure of two peacocks eating grain from the pot. Another gate attached to it has multifoliated arch.

39. Fransoo the author of *Tawarikh-i-Hunud*, 22a - 22b, 26b, authentically told the names of six wives of Suraj Mal, out of which one is Rani Ganga. She hailed from a village Bachchamadi in the present Bharatpur District and was the mother of Ranjit Singh whose unfinished cenotaph is still seen at Vrindaban.

Entering through it is a verandah, at the right of it is a passage which leads to the inner courtyard turning left. A window opens in the verandah towards the courtyard. The ground storey, which is on the land side as seen from the interior of the court, becomes a mere plinth for the support of a majestic double cloister with broad and lofty arch and massive clustered pier. From the inner court a few steps lead to the *chaupar* or *verandah*. May be the strangers were received in the verandah, children played or women sat or talk. In front of the courtyard is the place of worship. From the two corners of the courtyard the flight of stairs lead to the first floor.

On the first floor there are two verandahs on either side and a chamber. Four windows opens towards the main gate from the chamber. This may be the place where the rani used to reside. They are very very beautifully carved as seen from outside. These bow-shaped windows are beautifully designed. Now-a-days this is illegally occupied by the local residents. On this floor, at the left side, are three kiosks in a row having peculiar Bharatpur house design. The same pattern of double roof can be seen in it as in the pavilion on the second floor.

On the second floor is a *burj* at the back of the kunj. It is a very massive structure with a bow-shaped roof. The whole structure is built up of cream coloured stone. It has eight entrances in all. The pavilion is rectangular in shape with three gateways on either side and one each on opposite side. The three pairs of entrance has multifoliated arch while the other two have three foliated arches. The best part of this pavilion is its roof. It still glitters because of the mural paintings. The structure is at the top of the temple at the ground floor. In between the pavilion and the first storey is a gap *dochhatti* or it is a double roofed structure. This pavilion is also painted beautifully with the mural paintings from outside. At the time of its completion, this pavilion would have been very beautiful. Now it is not properly maintained and the paintings are fast withering away with time.

On this floor is a tank which may be used for water storage or may be connected with fountains to save oneself from the extreme heat. The eaves are beautifully carved. On either side of the back pavilion are four pair of windows with jali work, two of them are still surviving safely.

Towards the main gate are two pairs of windows enriched by jali work. They are designed in such a manner that the one peeping from inside could see all around without oneself to be seen. The pavilion at the front side, though much less massive than the back pavilion, is beautifully constructed. This rectangular pavilion has five pairs of gateways at opposite side out of which three pairs have multifoliated arch and the two pairs are built bow shaped. The stones are beautifully engraved in flowers, leafs and kangooras. It has four pairs of double columns which are beautifully carved. The bow shaped is not very high but it is decorated with mural paintings. In it mostly red and green colour is used for painting different types of decorative flowers. But on the roof of the two attached little chambers black and yellow colours are also used in the paintings with a different design. The chhajja of this pavilion is slanting.

The walls of the whole structure was polished in red and yellow. With the passage of time the polish slowly decayed and at present only traces are left to feel that at the time of its construction it would have been a gem in the heart of the holy land of Lord Krishna.

The pecularity of this kunj is its elegant designing, mural paintings and massive pavilion on the second floor at the back side. One of the drawbacks of this worth seeing structure is the disorderly placement of the stone slabs. Though mainly it is constructed of cream coloured stone, the red stones are also used here and there. The stones of the massive pavilion are of both colours which veils the beauty of this structure. Again the staircase at the second floor contains stairs of both the colours and likewise are the stones used at the top of the roof. May be the construction was completed in a quick time or lack of stones of the same colour was the cause of such a disorderly arrangement of somewhat excellent construction. Another pecularity is the double roof system; maybe to keep cool and to save from extreme heat the rani would have used this system. The style is the same which prevails at the Deeg palaces.

## Palaces in the Bharatpur Fort

There are three noteworthy palaces in the centre of the fort which were built by many generations. From the point of view of safety and security all the palaces in the fort were situated in the centre. They were constructed in a mixed style of Rajput and Mughals but in simplified form reflecting the Jats lack of ostentation. All the palaces are spacious and double storeyed having the bow-shaped roof with elegant balconies representing Mughal architecture. The following conclusion may be drawn—

**(i) Badan Singh's Palace**

Of the three palaces the main oriental wing of the palace is the oldest, being built by Raja Badan Singh who showed astonishing asthetic taste. The part of this palace is now with the museum. The hall is made up of marble. It was the venue of many historical events. On 5th February 1827 after the occupation of English army, the infant Raja Balwant Singh was placed on the throne of Bharatpur at the age of seven. His mother Ma Amrit Kaur was appointed as his regent and Jani Baijnath as the Diwan of the state. They were to rule in the presence of a British political agent. On that historic day, Lord Combermere and Sir Charles Matcalf were also present. Again on 18th March 1948, this hall proved to be the venue of the foundation of 'Matsya Union.'

**(ii) The Kamra Palace**

To the west, part of which is now with the museum is a big darbar hall of historical interest. It is situated in the Chaman Bagichi in the north of Rani Laxmi Palace. It previously housed the Bharatpur state armoury and treasury. This was the venue of all important darbars during the princely regime of Bharatpur. Rare pieces of architecture magnify the glory of 'Kamra Khas' which has been embellished with numerous items and articles of beauty imported from foreign countries.

**(iii) Mahal Khas**

To the east of Raja Badan Singh's palace was situated the Mahal Khas including the royal apartments built by Maharaja Balwant Singh (1826-53). This palace indicated the way of life of the royalty at the time. The rooms are comparatively small with stone cut lattice windows set in long arched alcoves. Many walls are still covered with multi-coloured, delicately painted designs in muted colours. The floor is of marble in various designs and colours. On the ground floor is the set of Turkish *hamams*, sunken baths for both cold and hot water. Some chambers are with split levels while the corner rooms are octagonal with round sun windows set in the centre of the domed ceiling. These rooms with painted walls and domed roofs are, along with the rest of the royal apartments, in strong contrast to much of this otherwise unadorned court.

## The State Museum

Primarily archaeological collection, this museum was founded in 1944 by Maharaja Sawai Brijendra Singh. While over-shadowed by the older and better known collections of Mathura and Agra it is certainly worth visiting.

It has some extremely interesting sculptures, including a late Gupta Shiv Parvati from the eight century, a Jain Tirthankara dated c.1020 and a 10th century Ganesh. Perhaps the most interesting piece is a second century redstone shivlinga. From the nearby village of Noh are terracota toys from the first to the third century Kushan period.

15. Badan Singh Kunj (Vrindaban)

16. Badi Kunj (Vrindaban)

17. Entrance Ganga Mohan Kunj (Vrindaban)

18. Mural painting on gateway (Ganga Mohan Kunj)

19. Bow shaped pavilion (Ganga Mohan Kunj)

20. Roof of the pavilion (Ganga Mohan Kunj)

21. Fading beauty (Ganga Mohan Kunj)

22. *Jharokha* used by royal ladies (Ganga Mohan Burj)

23. Main entrance (Laxmi Kunj)

24. Interior view (Laxmi Kunj)

## *Chapter 6*

# Other Secular Structures

### Gardens

In ancient times gardens known as *grhodyāna*, *bhavanodyāna* or *mandioradyāna* were adorned with leafy and flowery trees and garden pavilions. The lotus ponds were also a part of the garden complex with *krīdāparvataks*, the artificially raised mound for the pleasure resorts of the kings and the queens.

The garden plan was an essential feature of the town planning of Indo-Aryans.[1] The temples and *sālās* were provided with a perfectly layed out gardens with water channels. The water channels were essential components of garden planning. Certain trees and plants like *peepal*, *tulsi* etc. were considered as sacred as they have aesthetic and sanitory potentialities. Trees and plants in the well laid out garden not only serve the purpose of screening but also help in arresting the atmospheric pollution. Looking at the above factors garden planning formed an inseperable aspect of the palace complexes. *Krīdāudyana*, *Ashokavana*, *Shālavana* were a part of palace complex. Certain festivals like *Ashoka-Pusparachāyikā* and *Śālabhañjikā* were celebrated with great zeal in the city of Śravastī (district Bahraich, Uttar Pradesh).[2]

In ancient India, the celebration of such festivals speak volumes for the love of nature in general and gardens in particular. Vatsyayāna classified the gardens of the palaces viz. *pramododyānā* for the enjoyment of the kings and queens, *udyāna* for kings and their courtiers, *vrkshavātikā* for ministers and courtiers and lastly *nandanvana* dedicated to Lord Indra. The parks and sacred groves along with garden pavilions were meant for the general public.

In ancient India the geometric pattern was considered to be the best for town planning and hence according to *vāstupurus amaṇḍala* the same planning was followed in garden planning in the

1. A.P. Singh, *Forts and Fortifications of India*, p. 198.
2. A.P. Singh, *Forts and Fortifications of India*, p. 199.

palace complexes. The tradition of temple gardens travelled from India to the far east influencing the tradition of Japan and Chinese garden system. In Iran, its antiquity goes back to the time of Zennophone writing in 401 B.C. which describes how Cyrus the younger planted a garden with regular line of trees.[3] The Mughal gardens of India are the offshoots of the same tradition of ancient planning of gardens. The garden surrounding Humayun's mausoleum in Delhi and garden at Wair are surviving-examples. The *Baradaris,* the pillared pavilions, were part of ancient India's gardens. The following gardens laid out on the norms of geometric patterns testifying to the old Indian garden planning tradition with adequate supply of water are the garden at Humayun's Tomb, the Taj Mahal, gardens inside the fort of Agra and Delhi, Islamnagar fort, forts at Orchha (Tikamgarh), Narwar (Shivpuri) and the gardens inside the Jat palaces, specially at Deeg and Wair and the palaces in the South.

Early Hindu art revolved around the temple and the pantheon of deities. It was based on the concept of organic growth of the rhythms of nature and of humanity always complex and individual. Flowers and plants, especially the lotus, were a part of worship and were shown in intricate detail in the carvings. Much less is known of secular buildings and gardens, probably due to the devastating effects of natural calamities though there are traces of a contrasting geometry in the polygonal work of hill forts.

The Muslims by contrast brought with them a culture rooted in the desert and the oasis. It was compounded from abstract principles of order, mathemetics, law and above all from a profound belief in the unity of God. There designs were geometric, relying on calculated division and sub-division and upon enclosure from a hostile environment. In decoration flowers and calligraphy were woven into abstract patterns while colours were clear and brilliant.

The meeting of these two fundamentally different conceptions of life and art resulted in a fusion of Indo-Islamic themes from which the Mughals and much later the Jats enriched their own design in laying out gardens. The Tughlaqs had also built embankments, canals and gardens.[4] Some of the canals survived to be put to new uses by

---

3. R. Ali, *Islamic architecture in India after independence*, A Review of Research Bulletin of the Deccan college Research institution Vol. XXXVII No 14 Pune 1978, p. 113.
4. *The Gardens of Mughal India, A history and a guide*, p. 25, Vikas Publishing House, N. Delhi.

the forthcoming dynasties but of their gardens little but the memory remains.

It was the Mughals who took keen interest in laying out gardens. Being a man of high aesthetic taste, Babur felt delighted in creating beautiful *bags* (garden). Ahmad Yadgar writes : In the second year of his majesty's reign a beautiful garden was made on the borders of river Jamuna (Ram Bagh) at Agra.....he passed his time in that garden, in company with Mughal companions and friends, in pleasure and enjoyment and carousing, in the presence of enchanting dancing-girls with rosy cheeks, who sang tunes, and displayed their accomplishment.....[5] Mirza Kāmrāan also prepared a splendid garden similar to this in Lahore. When Humayun went to Persia in exile he visited all the palaces and gardens of Herat and admired them.[6]

The earlier Mughal garden-palaces perhaps derived their unique flavour from colours. The subtle low-toned red and yellows of the Hindus, the use of red sandstone and insets of black and white marble or blue schist made a considerable departure from the clear cut Persian colours. Hindu motifs appeared in such details as lintels, columns, eaves, fretled balconies or lotus roundels while carving was rich with flowers and animals, flower scrolls being combined with Muslim inscriptions.[7] Akbar's work at the Agra Fort was a 'tour de-force' of red sandstone, vigourously carved, while at Fatehpur Sikri much of the actual planning is casual and irregular, a far cry from Muslim concepts of order.

The Rajput heritage in designing the garden is perhaps most clearly seen at Amber, near Jaipur, the home of Akbar's Rajput wife and mother of Jahangir. Jahangir is credited to have designed a number of gardens, even in the beautiful valley of Kashmir.[8] These gardens with their romantic lake and hillside setting, their strange combination of the exact and picturesque, perfectly express the union of widely separated ideals. The stone parterres in the two important Amber gardens are based upon the star which was held in special esteem by the Seljuk Turks for whom it stood for life itself and for man's

5. Elliot and Dowson, *The History of India as told by its own Historians* volume V, p. 38.
6. S.R. Sharma, *Mughal Empire in India*, Karnataka Publishing House, 1940, p. 109.
7. *The Gardens of Mughal India* : A History and a guide, Vikas Publishing House Pvt. Ltd., p. 21.
8. *Shalamar Bagh*, *Achabal*; *Vernag*, and *Nishat Bag*.

intellectual powers. It may be significant that immigrants of Turkish origin had at one time taken refuge in Rajputana.

Later, the white marble architecture of Gujarat, one of Akbar's most important conquests, came to have an increasing impact until the central building in any important garden were almost always of white marble. Kashmir too extended its own special influences in the knowledge and use of flower decoration and atleast one Kashmiri name is recorded among the craftsmen of Taj Mahal.[9]

So, from different stands of different sub-cultures i.e. Indo-Islamic, Rajput, Gujarat, Kashmiri, the Great Mughal gardens evolved, with always predominantly the Persian connection linking the whole into an exquisite wholesome unit.

During the period of the decline of Mughals a large number of craftsmen, sculptures, labourers and masons migrated from Delhi to Agra and other nearby princely states in search of means of livelihood. The Bharatpur Kingdom provided the rare and much-needed blessings of a settled order, security of life and property. Badan Singh the founder ruler of the state exhibited astonishing asthetic tastes. He alone conceived the grand design of beautiful garden palaces with the help of men, money and material which were at his command. He and his son, Suraj Mal, used their newly-acquired wealth to create beautiful works of art. After Badan Singh's death, Suraj Mal's wealth and will galvanised the unprovided architects of the impoverished court of Delhi in the new home of the state of Bharatpur. Besides his forts, Suraj Mal, spent crores of rupees embellishing Deeg, Bharatpur, Wair and Kumher with 'Enchanting buildings, ponds and gardens'.[10]

The layout of the Jat Gardens is based on the Mughal horticulture plan called Char-Bagh. The notable characteristic of these gardens is their sunken appearance. The ornate stone flower-beds are usually absent. The most striking characater of these gardens is the task of producing artifical charms of water. The Jat architects achieved greater success in them than any one else.

The most beautiful and notable example are the garden palaces at Deeg. The grand garden retreat adorning this city is the most

---

9. *The Gardens of Mughal India*, p. 27.
10. *Tawarikh-i-Hunud* (Persian MS) 22a; also see *Dirgh* (Hindi MS), pp. 1-2, *Raspeeushnidhi*, in Somnath, p. 6, quoted by G.C. Dviwedi, *The Jats*, p. 260.

outstanding accomplishment of Jat rulers and serves to this day as a glorious memorial of Bharatpur State. At Wair, besides the fort, a large garden with a beautiful mansion was laid down called '*Safed Mahal*' and reservoirs in the centre called '*phulbari*'. The Sunken gardens were also constructed at Bharatpur Fort. The consorts of Raja Suraj Mal, Rani Kishori, Rani Hansia, Rani Mohini and Rani Laxmi are credited for laying down gardens throughout the state. Gobardhan, Vrindaban, Nandgaon, Kamar, Gunsara and Hansraj are the other notable places which were adorned with beautiful gardens. They are now withering away with time but still reflect the grandeur of the art of laying gardens by their rulers.[11]

## Gardens at Deeg

The Deeg gardens are square-shaped. The layout of the Deeg gardens is based on the Mughal horticulture plan known as the '*Chār-Bāgh*' or the fourfold garden pattern. Each plot is composed by four equal sized parterres produced by means of four canals radiating from a formal tank in the centre like the arms of a cross. A notable characteristic of the garden is the absence of ornate stone flower beds which plausibly was an outcome of the intention of designers to develop a thicker form of floriculture unlike thinly and more regularly planted flowers of the earlier gardens; yet while planting the trees they seem to have maintained the principle of discipline of the Mughal horticulture. Another characteristic of the palace-gardens is their conspicuous sunken appearance caused by deeper parterres and canals.

In the centre of the square occupied by the garden there is an octagonal cistern, 60 feet across, containing a group of jets surrounded by a paved walk. From this place the whole plan of the garden and the grouping of the buildings around it can be readily discerned. The raised pavements and the lines of fountains diverge thence to the middle of each of the four sides of the square and each quarter thus formed is again divided into plots intersecting in the centre of it.

The sides of the garden with the buildings parallel to them are exactly oriented along each of the cardinal points so that all the paths and fountains are aligned consequently either directly north and south or east and west. From the central octagon of the garden

11. At present these gardens are looked after by Archaeological Survey of India.

one line of fountain jets points north to the Nand Bhawan and south to the Kishan Bhawan while the intersecting line leads eastwards to the Gopal Bhawan and westwards to the Keshav Bhawan, a smaller pavilion placed at the end to balance the group.

The Jat architects succeeded in the task of producing artificial charms of water. Besides the canals and tanks, the major mediums of water display are fountains, cascades, chutes and the system of initiating beauties of the monsoon. The last named item, although a little fantastic, is originally and decidedly Indian in character. The idea itself was poetic and most probably derived from the anormous, literary tradition of the Braj-Bhasha.[12]

The Jat Rajas specially Badan Singh and Suraj Mal is credited to introduce the system of enjoying beauties of the monsoon rains. This clearly reflects the love of nature of the Jat rulers who did their best to achieve perfection in creating artificial charm combining the gardens with the romantic lakes and enjoying the artificial monsoon rain even in extreme heat.

The number of fountains are approximately 500 of both large and small sizes, closely set to each other. Most of these fountains

---

12. कैसे सावन में भाजे तुम आवते।
पपिहा 'पी' 'पी' जो यों गातो नहीं॥
धरती के प्यासे अधरन में जो कहूं।
प्यास न होती तो पावस आतो नहीं॥
तुम सजना हो प्यारे, ह्यां हर सांस के।
बरसौ बरसौ बादर, सावन मास के॥
जौ न कलाई सूनी होती नेह की।
इन्द्रधनुष कौ कंगना तो लातौ नहीं॥
कारे-कारे बदरन की करि छांव रे।
दुखियारी अंखियन पै यों छातो नहीं॥

(Shri Vishambhar Nath Upadhaya)
Braj Bharti, Bhadrapad, Samvat 2015
Varsh 16, Ang 4-5-6-
Prakashak Braj Sahitya Mandal Mathura.

यह पावस के रसवारे दिना, बदरा उमड़ै कजरारे घने।
लिखि अम्बर पै रहे प्रेम-कथा, गेहि की सुधि में हम बौरे बने॥
यह भेजते गान तुम्हारे तुम्हें, बदरा लपटाय हिये अपने।
बरसें सरसें तब आंगन में, सुभकामना के रस यों ये सने॥

(बाबूराम पालीवाल)
प्रकाशक ब्रज साहित्य मण्डल मथुरा।

have a sculptured floriferous body almost copying the patterns of the pillars existing here. In some cases there are arrangements for breaking the current of water into several small one (*budbuda*) by means of a basin with perforated bottom attached to a pipe-line, thus producing quiet a fanciful fountain inside the building.

A new type of cascade much more ornate than its previous examples can be noticed in at least two places. These are in the form of flower-shaped, semi-circular projections (*Kamal-Burgīs*) with a truncated top, on the front face of the terrace of the Gopāl Bhawan, where from the water was made to fall in the form of a thin and compressed sheet below, thereby creating a unique fascination.

The principal or the central garden of the palace complex has a *Chār-Bāgh* (fourfold) plan executed through four canals forming the pattern of a cross with a formal octagonal tank in the middle.

Each canal is provided with a small waterfall at the starting point. The parterres of the garden are surrounded by flagged footpaths which are connected with the buildings through comfortable ramps and flights of steps. A number of fountains arising from the beds of canals and tank heighten the pleasantness of the environment. The frontal projections of the terrace of the Nand Bhawan and Kishan Bhawan encroach upon a large portion of the garden but this arrangement creates a concord between the nature and architecture.

About the flora grown here there is nothing of special note but the position of certain trees suggests that the Mughal order of plantation was in vogue at one time, although characteristics of an Indian moon-light gardens also existed. The designers here appear to have successfully combined the system of the earlier Jal Mahal (Water Palace) with the scheme of a formal Mughal Garden.[13] The fairy work of Suraj Mal strengthens the harmony between architecture and gardens.

## Garden at Bharatpur Fort

In front of the palace complex built in Lohagarh fort lies a small but beautiful garden. The garden is square in shape and has a *Chār-Bāgh* (four fold) plan.

13. M.C. Joshi, *Dig*, New Delhi, 1971, p. 9.

The main characteristic of the garden is its clearly visible sunken appearance caused by the space of flower beds and canals. Another notable characteristic of the garden is the absence of ornate stone flower beds like the Wair Garden. The lines of fountains diverge to the middle of each of the floor sides of the square, and each quarter thus formed is divided into plots intersecting in the centre like the gardens at Deeg.

The main central wing of the palace which now houses a museum and the royal apartments in the right wing frames a picturesque scene of this sunken garden.

## Garden at Gunsara

Adjoining the tank is an extensive walled garden still memorising the art loving Rani Laxmi who built it beside the tank and Laxmi Kunj at Vrindaban.

The garden is rectangular in shape, the wall though falling in ruins at places is still standing. There are three gates (which are closed now) to enter, on the fourth side is a temple dedicated to Lord Krishna. In the centre of the garden is a beautifully carved plinth built up of cream coloured stone. This may be the sitting place for the queen to sit in the evening, to admire the natural surroundings. The plinth is kachcha at the top and at present shrubs are growing everywhere on it.

This extensive garden is about a thousand acres in extent. The water to the garden was supplied by a well and the masonry tank. The striking aspect of the vegetation is the presence of *Khirni* trees. Beside it *imli*, *neem*, *shisham*, *ashok* trees and vivid varieties of herbs and shrubs are present which all are in need of proper caring. The temple is in the garden itself. The garden on the large scale shows the love of Rani Laxmi towards gardens and greenery.

## Garden at Kamar

The town of Kamar lies in 27°49"N and 77°21"E at a distance of about six miles from Kosi. This place is famous for a walled garden at the outskirts of the town built by Raja Badan Singh.

This extensive garden is rectangular in shape. It is more than a thousand acres in extent. The garden is adorned with some monuments of the inlaws of Raja Badan Singh. The water to the garden is supplied from the surrounding woodland.

The garden is full of '*Khirni*', *pipal*, *mulbury*, *mehndi*, trees and bushes etc. This garden is in ruins now which needs a great rectification.

## Garden at Wair

Badan Singh's taste for architecture and aesthetic sense is testified by the remains of his numerous buildings, gardens and palaces. At Wair he planted within the fort a large garden with a beautiful house and reservoir in the centre called *phulbari*. This place was given by him to his son Pratap Singh who was a poet and lover of nature.

The garden at Wair was planned on the fourfold garden pattern. The parterres of the garden is provided with flagged footpaths. The raised footpaths and the lines of fountains[14] diverge to the middle of each of the four sides of the square and each quarter thus formed is again divided into plots intersecting in the centre of it. On one of the raised causeways is a stone platform or *chabutra* built of cream coloured stone from which the king could enjoy the spectacle of the spring blossom on the fruit trees and compose his poem. The *chabutra* would probably have been covered with a carpet and a rich cover of canvas to give protection from the sun.

The chief charateristic of the *phulbari* is the presence of ornate stone flower beds which was the outcome of the intention of the designers to develop a thick form of horticulture.

At the juncture of the garden and Safed Mahal is a square cistern. It might have contained a group of jets and water in the past but now it is used as volleyball ground.

The garden at Wair not only reflects the Mughal influence but also the Rajput heritage which is perhaps most clearly seen at phulbari. This garden, with their romantic lake and hillside settings, their strange combination of the exact and the picturesque, perfectly express the union of widely seperated ideals.

---

14. Fountains are no more seen in *phulbari* except the holes in which they were fitted.

Besides these beautiful gardens, the Jat kings also built tanks, dams and *ghats* for various purposes. Besides utilitarian aspects, they reflect the imperial glory and no doubt are the manifestations of Jat aesthetics. The desert climate of neighbouring states of Rajputana, scarcity of drinking water and dependence of rainfed agriculture probably forced them to construct tanks and dams. The concept and structural design however, are exquisite.

# Tanks

### Tanks at Deeg

## The Rup Sagar

This magnificant reservoir was built by Rup Singh, the brother of Raja Badan Singh, at the instance of his spritual guru in the hope of obtaining descendants because he was then childless.

Generally called *Pakka Tālāb*, it is among the earlier structure built at Deeg. The tank measures 82 m. square and the depth of water is about 6 m.

Each side of it has two pairs of buttresses ending with octagonal bastions marking the bottom edge of the steps. The long necks of the buttresses serve as screens to the bathers. The treatment of this kind strengthenes the fabric and enlivens the architecture.[15] If the work had been quite finished cupolas would have been mounted on these bastions. The most outstanding structural feature in this tank is noticeable in its surrounding bathing ghats.

It may be added that Rup Singh's hopes were not fullfilled but his priest consoled him by pointing out that the Rup Sagar would sufficiently perpetuate his name.

## The Gopal Sagar

Generally called Kacha Tālāb, this tank is designed as oblong. The maximum depth of it is stated to be about 6m, the same as that of the Rup Sagar. Till 1866 this reservoir had earthern exbankments and even now the western side, opposite the Gopal Bhawan, is in original state.

Easy stair ghats with ornamental walls have, since then, been constructed on the north and south of the tank and the open space

15. M.C. Joshi, *Dig*, p. 29.

has been filled with a beautiful evergreen garden. Only the western side of the tank now remain kacha and it has been sloped off and turfed and at the northern end of it an ornamental bridge has been built over a gap which makes it an excellent cattle ghat.

## The Water Reservoir

On the west of the Kishan Bhawan, at the level of its roof, is a water reservoir supported on arches which are hidden by the blank outer wall facing the garden.

There is an easy ramp leading up to the top. This reservoir is about 35 feet high above the terrace. This measures about 40.85 by 31.70 m and it was usually filled about 2m deep thus having a vast capacity.

The purpose of erecting the tank at such a height was only to operate the fountains, chutes and cascades within the building and gardens in the best possible way.[16]

For filling this reservoir, four wells are built in the vicinity and the water from them was lifted up from these wells by means of leather buckets drawns by bullocks. The cistern in older days could be filled in about a week's time; and when all the fountains are playing at once, the water runs out in few hours.

The water supply to different fountains was regulated by numerous holes on its walls which form the mouths of various pipe lines connected with different groups of fountains. The system of using them was kept a closely guarded secret in those days.

# Tanks at Govardhan

## Kusum Sarovar

This magnificent artificial lake is situated at a short distance from Govardhan. It is on the margin of this reservoir that the famous *chhattri* of Raja Suraj Mal was erected by his son Raja Jawahar Singh.

The Kusum Sarovar is 460 feet square. The outstanding structural feature in this artificial lake are the flight of stone steps built of cream coloured stone, each side being broken into one central and four smaller side compartments by panelled and arcaded wall running out 60 feet in water. The side compartments are in the shape of bold gallaried projections with an octagonal face.

---

16. M.C. Joshi, *Dig*, p. 24.

It is said that it was dug by Bir Singh Bundela but renovated and erected in the present shape by Jawahar Singh.

The name of this tank is related to the legend of Vajranabha's encounter with Uddhava (cf. 2.40). The appearance in literary sources of Kusum Sarover (flower pond) or some synonymous variant of the name, suggests that it was a recognized location before it was provided with masonry steps.[17]

The northern side of the sarovar, the ghat of the lake, is partly in ruins and it is said were reduced to this condition a very few years after its completion by the Gosain Himmat Bahadur, who carried away the materials to Vrindaban to be used in the construction of a ghat which still commemorates his name there.[18]

All the four sides of the sarovar are furnished with good ghats which appear quite impressive. Till today this construction in the land of Lord Krishna provides water and shelter from scorching sun to the devoted pilgrims who pass this way.

## PanchTirth kund

Panchtirth Kund, believed to incorporate five celebrated bathing places (Ganges, Gaya, Kurukshetra, Prayag and Pushkar) is said by some local scholars to be the tank in front of the two *chhattris* of Baldev Singh and Balwant Singh, opposite the Laxmi Narayan Temple. This is more or less in agreement with '*Bhuśundiramāyanā*', which says that it lies at the same place as *chakratirtha*.[19]

This tank is constructed on the pattern of Kusum Sarovar. The tank is somewhat square in shape and about 6 m in depth. It is built of cream coloured stone. It is composed of noble flight of stairs and looks picturesque because of the bathing *ghats* in all direction. The backside of Balwant Singh's cenotaph and the side of Baldeo Singh's *chhattri* with their numerous arched gateways of fine architecture possesses a grandeur scarcely perceptible in any other building while it is very agreeable scene to look at the tank and the garden beyond from these *chhattries*.

Beneath the cenotaph of Balwant Singh are two semi octagonal projections with no kiosks. A pavilion is also built on this side. A pavilion is also constructed in Baldeo Singh's *chhattri*. The water in

---

17. A.W. Entwistle, *Braj Centre of Krishna - Pilgrimage*, p. 348.
18. F.S. Growse, *A District Memoir*, p. 308.
19. A.W. Entwistle, *Braj Centre of Krishna - Pilgrimage*, p. 300.

the tank is passed through two arched gateways almost fully immersed in the water.

This tank is in need of renovation. The pavilion beneath Balwant Singh's *chattri* is about to fall. This religious pond which still commemorate the architectural merit of Jat rulers should be maintained and preserved.

## Tank at Parsoli - (Chandra Sarovar)

The village of Parsoli, renamed Mohammadpur during the Mughal period, lies 3 miles on the road from Goverdhan to Sonkh. In the *vārtā* literature Parsoli is said to be the village where Surdas lived.

On the opposite side of the Govardhan-Sonkh road is a large tank called Chandra Sarovar. *Pushtimarg* sources relate this place to the tradition of Lord Krishna who stayed the moon to stay for a night lasting six months so that he could enjoy the *rās* with the *gopies.*[20] It is said that this pond is somewhat 5,000 years old. In performing *Maha Rās* Lord Krishna's sweat converted into this pond.

'इत उत गोपी, बिच बिच माधव। निरतत ताता थेई।'

Vrindaban Chandradas describes the tank as circular and contains water that resembles moonlight.

*Chādanī Sau Jala Chandramā Sau Chakrākāra Kuṇda.*

Present Chandra Sarovar is in fact octagonal in shape constructed by Raja Jawahar Singh. It is enclosed with masonry steps built by Raja Nahar Singh and restored by Raja Jawahar Singh in 1754. Rani Hansia also renovated a part of it and built a temple constructed in the form of a moon, there is also a water palace in this eightfold sarovar. Earlier it was surrounded by *kadam trees* and a big *bat vraksh* known as *Vanshi Bat.*[21]

## Tank at Gunsara

On the road leading to Kumher from Sonkh, at a distance of about two kms., on the left, just across the Bharatpur border is a very fine masonry tank worthy of a visit from anyone in the neighbourhood.

---

20. Gopal Prasad Vyas, *Vrindaban*, p. 230.

21. F.S. Growse, *Mathura : A District Memoir*, p. 234.

The tank is built on the same scale and the same style as the Kusum Sarovar near Goverdhan. This was constructed by Rani Laxmi, the consort of Raja Randhir Singh, who built Laxmi Kunj at Vrindaban.

The tank is square in shape on each side the flight of the steps is broken into two divisions by bold gallerried projections with octagonal face. These octagonal bastions mark the bottom edge of the steps. The long gallaries serve as screen to the bathers. The tank is furnished by good bathing ghats which enlivens the architecture.

To this tank is connected a well and a beautiful garden with a temple inside it. On one side of this tank are three chambers each having three gates. They are built in peculiar Jat style.

The tank was not quite completed at the time of Rani Laxmi's death and has never been touched since then. The villagers enjoy this tank which is still full of water about 6m deep. But slowly and steadily it is ruining because of the lack of renovation. This beautiful piece of Jat architecture should be restored and utilized at the time of summer.

## Jawahar Kund

To the south-west of Kusum Sarovar, to the left, is a masonry tank Jawahar Kund, named after Raja Jawahar Singh. This is simple and is not on such a large scale as the other tanks.

The tank is square in shape. It is built of red sandstone. On all the four sides are projections with semi octagonal face. It has no architectural merit but still commemorates the building achievements of Raja Jawahar Singh.

## Bihar Sagar at Agra

This *pakka tālāb* was constructed by Jani Behari Lal, diwan of the Bharatpur darbar. This tank is square in shape and is about 4m in depth. This tank is constructed in Balka Basti very near to the ancient temple of Shri Mangleshwar Nath.

Now in a dilapidated state and suffering from unauthorised possession, this tank was at one time the fairest jewel in the garland of monuments.

The gateway is beautifully designed with fairies and lion. The sun mark of Bharatpur State on the doorway still glitters. This gate is made of cream coloured stone and an inscription is engarved on it which reads "Serving so long such royal chief as H.H. well named Yashwant Singh some lasting blessing to secure a sincere well wishes of all, Jani Nathni Ramji's son by caste a *Vad* Naura Nagar has coterected here for all, under the king supervision Bhatt Bal Mukund the head pandit, Bhatt Jagnnath Ji's only son in eighteen hundred and ninty two to Bharatpur the native place. At Agra his place of learning viz. English, Arabic,Urdoo (urdu). As his each composition shews (shows) may this be ever charming all. Amen, Amen, Amen."

On the right side of the gate is another inscription which reads—

> "Her majesty's much loyal (?) the son of well famed Balwant Singh P.S. Head V. of Bharatpur R.B.D.J. Behari Lall the youngest and unmarried one. Shri Mangleshwar Behar Sagar submitting to their friendly call of public good desiring one. In Agra college of Sanskrit family fame increasing one on his returning from Abu to shew (show) here the relative grace. Good means of subsistence earring Persian, Sanskrit, Hindi too. How much he to its college owes. As bliss he never harming all, inspired secretly, greets the pen. "

On the corners of the tank are four kiosks built up of the same stone. The kiosks are somewhat massive and duly shows the strength. Two of the kiosks at present are in unauthorised possession. They have placed bricks to convert them into the room.

Besides the main gate, the tank has three more small passages on each side. On the passage to the left of the main gate is engraved an inscription in Braj dialect which reads—

**श्री हरि :**

श्री मड़लेश्वर बिहार सागर

भरतपुर के महाराजाधिराज महाराज ब्रजेन्द्र सिंह यशवंत सिंह बहादुर, बहादुर जंग जी. एस. आई. की भक्तिपूर्वक सेवा का फल

**छंद :** श्री हटकेश्वर इस्ट अनुग्रह, सबअभीष्ट में पूरणा मंगलेश्वर बिहार सागर श्रुघ् यहु वन भयौ सू पूरण॥ चहुं दिश घाट सुघाट मनोहर, बिमल नीर नल पूरित। मनहु कलिंदी लहर नदी , आई कलिमल भूरित -।

सज्जन साधु संत भज्जन कर, पूज महेशहि हर्ष। खग भृग तरू तर कीड़हि जल जल पा, सुमन सुन आकशै॥ धनी रात दीवान बिहारी लाल वकिल वनिवायौ॥

संवत नव श्रुति प्रंक चन्द्र में, सुजस चन्द्रवत धायौ - 2

**दोहा :**

अब पितु भ्राता जाति कुल, गुण पदवी परिवार। कमर सरोवर बनन कौ हेतु मकत निरधार - 3

ज्ञानी नथनीराम द्विज, बड़नगरा श्रीमान। नागर गुण सागर भये, तिन सुत चार सुजान - 4

झगन लाल जी प्रथम ही, दूजे छन्नू लाल, तीजे परमानंद मल मगन रहे कुंजलाल - 5

चौथे यह सब से लघू, यै गुण माँहि विशाल। रा. दी. जा. व. पं. सं. सपद, विदित बिहारी लाल - 6

ज्ञानी कुल पदवी रही, कच्छ दिवानि दीवान, भरतपुरषित वीर के, रहे वकील प्रधान -7

रहै रेजीडेनी जहां, आबू, मुख्य स्थान, बहुर पंच सरदार किय, श्री ब्रजेन्द्र सनमान - 8

राव बहादुर की बड़ी, पदवी जुबली माहि, केसर महाराणी देई, जिन प्रताप पहुंचाहि - 9

इभि वैभव सम्पत पद, पाय जित्यो इन काम। व्याहन कीनौ आपनो अंगन परस्यो वाम - 10

रहे ब्रह्मचारी तऊ, गहे गृही पन ढंग। विद्या पटरानी सहित सब उपाधि रही संग - 11

ओरहु इनके उर वसी, विविध विदेसिनितीय। इंग्लिश, अरबी, फारसी, उर्दू रूंचिरमणीय - 12

देसी संस्कृत नागरी, लख नागर नवरंग। सवति भावत तंजि सकल शुचि, विरचति नवल प्रसंग - 13

प्रकटे सुत सद्रन्थ बहु, छयो सुजस संसार। विशद बिहारी लाल कृत, यह अपूर्व परिवार - 14

रेजीडेंट साहिब चले, राज पर्य्यन हेतु। तब आबू से भरतपुर, आय रहे स्व निकेत - 15

जरा बिवस मन शिथिल लख, सुमति कस्या सुविचार। जन्मस्थान यहै वन्यो, पै अध्ययन उपचार - 16

तैजुं आगरे मैं, किर्या, तहुं करि कछु उपकार। ये मति अनुमति मानचित्र, हित साधारण धार - 17

बल्का की बस्ती निकट, श्री मंगलेश्वर नाथ। परम रम्भ मंदिर जहां, सबहि नवावै माथ - 18

अति पुनीत थलणय यह, सागर रचना कीन। पंडित बाल मुकन्द भट, हस्तै वन्यो नगीन - 19

बर्नत सुबुध जान बिहारीलाल सहस्त्रौ दिच यहै। चिरकाल कीर्ति बिहार सागर श्रुचि, सलिल पूरित रहै - 20

The noble flights of the tank is made of red sandstone which goes down to the centre. The water was poured in from the well just outside the tank; outlets can be seen at the steps.

There is need of renovation of this historical tank which is one of the rarely found pakka tālāb in Agra region.

## Tank at Saḥar

The town of Sahar is situated in 27°33' N and 77°33' E, at a distance of about 21 miles from Mathura.

It is famous for the large masonry tank adjoining the handsome house. This tank was constructed by Raja Badan Singh. One side of this tank is faced with stone and the rest is left unfinished. Probably the death of Badan Singh interrupted the work which is still lying in the same state.

## DAMS

Dams or barrages are strong walls built across a river to hold back the flow of water. They can be just a couple of six-foot logs that are used to dam up a tiny brook trickling through the backyard or a great block of dazzling white concrete rising into the sky and stretching as far as fifteen football fields. For thousand of years men have built dams to make sure they had reservoirs of drinking and irrigation water.

Dams are made of timber, rock, earth, masonry, or concrete or of combinations of these materials. Timber dams are seldom used because they do not last long and their height is limited. Rock fill dams consists of an embankment of loose rock with either a core impervious to water or a water tight face on the upstream side. Earth dams may be either simple embankments of earth or embankments reinforced with a core of cement or with an upstream surface made water tight. Masonry and concrete dams are either gravity dams (those dependent upon their own weight for resistance to the pressure of the water) or arch dams (either single - arch or multiple - arch dams). Single - arch dams are horizontally curved upstream and are usually constructed in narrow canyons or gorges where the rocky side walls are strong enough to withstand the tremendous thrust of the dam. Some dams are of the multiple - arch type, consiting of a number of single arches supported by buttresses.

Dams have from early times been constructed to provide a ready supply of water for irrigation and other purposes. The other main purposes of the dam was to provide water for irrigation, to aid flood control and to improve the navigability of waterways.

One of the earliest large dams to supply a ready supply of water and irrigation was a marble structure built by Rana Raj Singh in Rajputana[22] (Rajasthan) in c. 1660.

The founder ruler of Bharatpur State, Badan Singh, and his son, Suraj Mal, were aware of the water problem arising from the geographical situation of their newly acquired territory. Only seasonal rivers, Ruparel, Banganga and Kakunda flowed from their empire. In order to supply water to the Bharatpur fort and the defensive ditch around it they built a Bund on river Ruparel called Moti Sagar Bund. The Bharatpur rulers built more than 100 petty dams beside the Bund Baretha dam in order to maintain a proper supply of water for irrigation and drinking at different places in their territory like Rarah, Chimuti etc.

Bund Baretha has been included because it is the only live dam and is an outstanding example. This dam still provides drinking water to present Bharatpur city which was once the capital of Jat kingdom.

## Bund Baretha

It appears that its original name was Vairat.[23] Here the ruler of Bharatpur constructed a dam. This place is situated about 57 km

---

22. *The Columbia Encyclopedia*, p. 502; edited by William Bridgwater and Elizabeth J. Sherwood, Columbia University Press, Morningside Heights, New York, 1950.
23. *BrajendraVansh Bhaskar*, p. 190.

from Bharatpur and nine km from Bayana. Its construction was completed in 1897.

The dam is situated at the distance of approximately two and a half km from the railway station. The sight of it is very picturesque. Beautiful rocky hillocks on both the side with huge quantity of preserved water makes the heart fill with Joy. Besides it, it helps the inhabitants settled round about by supplying water and saving them from the fierce flood of the Kakunda river. There are two barriers to help in accumulating water. Both these barriers have over it small pavilions with three multifoliated arches built of red sandstone. Ahead of them is a kiosk each, beneath it are the barriers. In between the water barriers is a kiosk built of red sandstone in which it has a similar kiosk with beautiful inverted lotus flower on which an inscription is engraved in marble. The base of this kiosk is beautifully and elegantly engraved. The inscription reads that—

*Bharatpur State*
*Baretha Bund*

*Commenced A.D. 1866 by Captain Home R.E. during the minority of Maharaja Jaswant Singh of Bhurtpore and abandoned incomplete on his accension A.D. 1867.*

*The portion of the dam across the river bed not having been completed.*

*The work was recommenced A.D., 1896*
*according to a revised design*
*in the time of*

*H.H. Maharaja Ram Singh and Col. Loch Political Agent and was completed in time to catch the floods of A.D. 1897.*

*During the scarcity of A.D. 1897 about 3,000 people were employed daily on the work.*

*Executive Engineer J.A. Devenish, ESQ RE*

*Overseers in charge of work, Mr. Allah Bux, and Chooni Lall*

*Petty contractors, Alla Beli, Mola Bux etc. of Ajmere.*

This incription is engraved in Hindi, English and Urdu. The inscription shows that the dam was completed in two phases. During the first spell in 1866 A.D. the portion of the dam across the river bed was not tried. But the pressing need in 1896 A.D. of the flood made Maharaja Ram Singh to think for its completion. The work was started on the grand scale in order to complete it in time to catch the floods of 1897 A.D. The construction was commenced at the time of scarcity. About 3,000 unemployed people were employed daily on the work. The day and night work on the construction completed it in time. The work was completed on the contract basis. Petty contractors were called from far off places like Ajmer etc. The executive engineer was J.A. Devenish who had a deep knowledge in the field of architecture.

It is a unique irrigation structure to impound water and then to use it in a optimum way for irrigation and water supply purposes. This dam is constructed at a most suitable site i.e. most economical to trap the water of "Kakunda" river having the catchment area of about 70 sq. miles. It has been constructed in a valley with mountains and hillocks on either side. The third side has been blocked, firstly, by a trapezoidal shaped earthern bund and then by providing a stone pitching to add extra strength to the bund.

There are three passages for the stored river water. Firstly, there is a eight panel regulator constructed on the river which is kept generally closed except in severe flood situations. Secondly, there is a surplus water bund provided with sluice gates. The water passing through this passage is carried away by an escape which is finally discharged into river Yamuna. The third and the final passage was and is being used for irrigation and water supply purposes for the Bharatpur town. Still today the town of Bharatpur is fed with this water after giving the necessary treatment.

The sluice gates are operated by rotating the spindle in clock wise and anticlock wise direction. The chamber of the passages are constructed by the locally available stones. The walls near the base are wider and have been reduced to thickness by giving suitable offsets to sustain the available earth pressure. Splayed and straight wing walls are used to collect water from the dam.

An inscription is engraved on the kiosks of the sluice gate which reads thus—

*Bharatpur State*
*Baretha Bund*
*Assumed Reduced level*

*Top of Core Wall-690.00*
*Top of Bank Inside 687.00*

*Top of Bank Outside -685.00*
*Sluice no.1 West (Sill of lower shutters-651.00*
*(Sill of upper shutters-660-00*
*Sluice no. 2 - sill of shutter floor-662.50*
*Bed of channel no. 1 - At Head-650.00*
*Bed of channel no. 2 - At Head-662.00*
*Bed of channel no. 3 - At Head-655.00*
*Escape level........ -680.00*
*Lowest Bed of stream............ -635.00*

*Another inscription is also engraved on the cream coloured stone kiosk which dealt in detail regarding the level of contours, the area of water spread and the capacity of the water. The inscription thus sates—*

| *Reduced Level contours* | *Measured sq. miles* | *Water spread bighas* | *Calculated million* | *Capacity cubic feet* |
|---|---|---|---|---|
| *660.00* | *3/4* | *1200* | | *15.3* |
| *670* | *2.1/4* | *3500* | *418* | *1830* |
| *675.00* | *3* | *4800* | *365* | *1890* |
| *Escape Level at* | | | | |
| *680.00* | *3-3/4* | *6050* | *472* | *1568* |
| *682.00* | *4.1/2* | *7300* | *232* | *1800* |
| *H.F.L. of 1889 A.D.* | | | | |

## Note

One Bigha = 2/3 Acre

This dam is the biggest dam in Bharatpur State out of approximately 300 dams both large, medium and small sized. This work of the Bharatpur rulers, gratified their asthetic sense and emphasized their splendour but also shows their kindness, love and affection which they had for their subjects.

## Ghats

Another classic example of Jat architecture is the execution of ghats on the river Yamuna. Construction of the ghats on the river banks is an object of architectural magnificence peculiar to India.

The ghats constructed by Bharatpur rulers may be taken as a fair specimen of the class, although many are richer and much more elaborately adorned. The aim of these ghats is to afford easy access to bathers, by the flight of slabs in front of the river. Besides their religious and cultural significance they also prevented the cutting of enhancements by the river and also soil erosion which could have threatened human lives.

## Kesi Ghat at Vrindavan

This is one of the most sacred ghats. This was constructed by Rani Laxmi, the consort of Raja Randhir Singh. It is built up of cream coloured stone. This ghat is broken by small projections which is crowned by kiosks, which take off the monotony inherent in long lines of narrow steps.

The flight of stairs is backed by Laxmi Kunj which is a peculiar object of architectural display. This ghat is at present in a bad shape. Heaps of dirt and filth can be seen all around this holy ghat. Unfortunately the river has changed its course some fifty years back. It was planned many time to bring it back to the original place. Amount of rupees one lakh was collected by 'Shri Yamuna Sangrakshni Sabha'. A canal was dug at the side of the river but due to the technical fault made by the engineer this plan failed. In 1952 the river came to the Kesi Ghat but then the accumulated sand became hindrance to the smooth flowing. The students of Prem Vidyalaya[24], Shri Narayan Das, Shri Ram Nath Ji Vyas etc. worked assiduosly to make the river flow from the ghat. In 1953 the Yamuna river flowed from six ghats including the Kesi Ghat.

## Ghat at Hansganj[25]

This ghat built by Rani Hansia, the consort of Raja Suraj Mal, is now in a dilapidated condition. Two types of stones are used for the construction of steps. Steps in front of the river Yamuna are built of Red Stone while the stairs at upper side of cream coloured stones.

The ghat is backed by a building. It is merely an object of

---

24. Prem Vidyalaya started by Raja Mahendra Pratap is situated at Kesi Ghat.
25. Hansganj Ghat and the village was founded by Rani Hansia. It lies at the other side of the holy city Mathura.

architectural display without any particular destination, except to afford shelter from the sun rays. This is popularly known as tebari in Braj region.

The ghat is broken by two small projections which are crowned by kiosks. These kiosks are somewhat completely broken but the facade supporting it can still be seen. Built of cream coloured stone they are beautifully carved.

The enclosed chamber had three multifoliated arched gates. There are shelves in it, which may be used for keeping belongings. The pillars are made up of red stone. This ghat was damaged in the floods of 1978.

Thus, we see that the Jat rulers of Bharatpur laid down an important tradition of architecture which influenced the socio-cultural life of the people. They were not only embodiments of Indian cultural ethos but also carved a niche for themselves by erecting beautiful buildings, gorgeous gardens, exquisite and utilitarian tanks, bunds and ghats.

25. Tank at Gunsara with gallaried projections

26. Cream coloured plinth in the garden at Gunsara

27. View of Kusum Sarovar, waiting for renovation

28. Jawahir Kund

33. General view of Kesi Ghat

34. Broken stairs and projections at Kesi Ghat

# Chapter 7
# Religious Buildings

## Temples

Sacred spots, where nature was at her best or where some extraordinary event took place, became sites for temples built to honour different deities. Due to the Brahmanic influence legends and supernatural happenings were associated with them. The earliest temples were found to consist only of very simple cubical cells, probably built of wood and mud plaster with bamboo thatch-roofing. Gradually temples were hewn out of rocks, built of stones and of bricks according to the resources of the locality. Wood and stone were the best materials which suited constructions under the classic trabeated order. In brick it was not so easy to produce the horizontal styles of work without restoring to frequent and crowded intermediate supports.[1]

India has been the home of a great civilization for 5,000 years or more. Like her mighty rivers her civilization too has absorbed, century after century, many tributaries of culture, varied traditions, customs and moves, some turbid and others pure. The main under current was always Indian. Its literature, religion, philosophy, art and architecture have all retained their basic Indianness to a degree that has bordered oddly on the insular. The Indian temple, both as an institution and as architecture, is a product of this insularity. Hindu art and architecture have progressed along tracks cut entirely by indigenous talent. Islam which exercised a powerful and long standing influence on the ideas and institutions of the country from the 13th century onwards could do little to change the traditional character of temple architecture. India's earlier contacts with modern Europe were hardly noteworthy for their so called civilizing or cultural influence. The Indian temple has remained a typically Indian institution, as indigenous as the parthenon of Athens or the pyramids of Egypt.

---

1. *Indian Architecture, Vol. II Architectonics*, Edited by M.S. Anathalwar and Alexander Rea, compiler A.V. Thiagaraja Iyer. Page 338. Indian Book Gallery.

Indian temple is phenomenon of an age of faith. The imposing, structures were built mostly between 900 and 1600 A.D. Before and after this period many notable temples were built and carved but they represent only the earlier and later phases of a grand movement. South Indian temples are unparalleled example of the intermingling of mystic spirituality and the celestial. They are commemoratives as well as devotional. They reflect the best and the most of contemporary society.

An Indian temple is not necessarily a Hindu shrine. It can belong to any of the several religious denominations-Buddhist, Hindu, Jain or Sikh. Barring Sikh temples where the only object of veneration is the sacred book-*Guru Granth Saheb*-all others are built to enshrine the images of gods, goddesses or saints.

Before going deep into the architecture of Jat temples it is necessary to define the principal parts of a temple. The first and important part is the *garbha-griha*, meaning womb-cell. It is a dark, small square cell, where the main deity invariably carved in stone, is installed. On the roof of this cell rises the *shikhar* or tower also called the *vimana*. The doorway of the sanctum which always faces eastward opens into another rectangular chamber which is called the *antarala* or vestibule. The vestibule is the intermediate chamber between the sanctum and a pillared hall called *mandapa* where devotees gather at the time of worship. Entrance to the *mandapa* is by a porch called *ardha-mandapa*. In a fully formed temple there may be a transept on each side of the central hall known as the *maha-mandapa*. All around the sanctum is a passage meant for circumambulation by the worshippers. It is common for most of the big temples to be provided with an enclosing wall, some of them, the more elaborate ones, have a cloistered setting with many cells running right round the enclosing wall and facing the temple.[2]

The upward thrust of the sanctum tower was symbolic of its spiritual eminence. While the tower loudly announced the presence of God, at close range the temple overwhelmed the faithful by the variety and wealth of carving on its walls, pillars and ceilings. The temple itself became one enormous piece of sculpture and its architectural features were often subordinated to the carvers' skill. Figures of gods and goddesses, lovely maidens, floral motifs,

---

2. *Temples of India*, published by Publication Division, Ministry of Information and Broadcasting, Government of India, p. 8.

elephants, chariots horses, battle scenes, dwarfs and demons, stories from legends and myths and often enough provocative erotic themes - all these sought to picture before the faithful the righteous ways of the god and sins of evil-doers.[3] In short, the religious faith that the architecture of the temple evokes, does not spring from a cynical denial of life but from its warmest depths. In the presentation of this idea the Hindu temple builder was content to be governed by established conventions rather than by his inventive genius. And Jat temples were no exception.

## Temple of Nand Baba at Nandgaon

The village of Nandgaon is situated about 40 kms. north-west of Mathura and about 12 kms. west from the town of Chhata, it lies in 27°43' N and 77°23' E at the foot of Nandishwar hill about 8 kms from Barsana.

This town of temples is renowned for possessing temple of Nand Baba. It is the finest and the most sacred of temples. The temple is situated on the eastern side of the Nandishwar mountain on a high platform. This temple was founded by Rup Singh brother of Badan Singh who was a Sinsinwar jat at about 1750 A.D.

The temple stands in the centre of a paved courtyard. Its door is faced towards the west which goes against the established norms of Hindu culture and principles of Hindu temple architecture. The walls and roof of the temple are beautifully painted. The paintings consists of the *Bal Lila* of Lord Krishna and Balram. In front of the *Garbh Garha* is the idol of Jag Mohan. At the right of Mata Yashoda is the idol of Rajeshwari Shri Radha Rani. At the back of Nand Baba can be seen the *Jhanki* of Bal Gopal, such *Jhanki* as depicted in the temple is very rare in India. The idol of Nand Rai is not very old. This was brought from Jaipur and established here some 50 or 60 years ago.

At the outset, the temple was situated in a cave at Hills.[4] The temple at present is surrounded by a circular lofty wall with four corner kiosks. These command extensive view of Bharatpur hill and the level expanse of the Mathura district as far as Govardhan.[5] These

3. *Temples of India*, p. 9.
4. Pt. Premdatta Mishra Maithil, p. 190.
5. F.S. Growse, *Mathura: A District Memoir*, p. 315.

kiosks may have been used to announce the sacred activities in the temple.[6] From these kiosks the *pandas* (religious guides) introduce the *kund* to the pilgrims who visit this holy shrine. The temple consists of an open nave, with choir and sacrarium beyond, the latter being flanked on either side by a *rasoi* and a *Sej Mahal* (cooking and sleeping apartment), and has two *Skikhars* or towers.

The temple has an endowment of 826 Bighas of rent free land which remains distributed among Goswami *pujari's* or priests. The *Bhog* is arranged by the *Seths*. *Bateri* serves the temple according to their turn.

Workship is divided into *Dehris*. Both the gates of the temple are huge and are beautifully designed. At the front of both the gates are small *pori's*. After visiting the temple, pilgrims sit there and experience peace and pleasure. A couplet is famous about the *pori* -

सिंह पोरी को बैठिबो, पावन के स्नान।
झांकी बाबा नंद की, सहज मिले भगवान।[7]

At the *Parikarma Marg*, on the left (perimeter of the temple), is a small temple of Nandishwar Mahadev. The temple, though large, is in a clumsy style of architecture. It is the most sacred temple of Nandgaon, magnificantly constructed, historically important though not of much architectural importance.

## Vrindaban

### Kishori Mohan Temple[8]

It was built by Rani Kishori, the consort of Maharaja Suraj Mal, who dedicated it to Kishori Mohan (Radha & Krishna).

The shrine is on the right of the entrance on a plinth about 3 meters in height. The usual cream coloured stone is used in the construction. There is a verandah in front of the *Garbh Griha*. There are two rooms on either side. A flight of steps lead to the upper *tebari* (Goakh) from both the sides. The front wall of the temple is now white washed. The roof is made of slabs of the cream coloured

6. Pt. Premdatta Mishra Maithil, p. 190.
7. *Ibid*., p. 190.
8. Information regarding the temple was provided by Pt. Chandra Bhan Misra son of Mahant (at present) - Pandit Kaushal Kishore Mishra.
   The temple opens from 9 to 12 A.M. and 5 to 9 P.M.

stone. Infront of it is a square courtyard. About a foot raised platform in the centre of the courtyard is a *tulsi gamla*. An inscription on a square marble slab says: *Kishori Rani Kunj, Mohalla Radha Raman Vrindaban, Kishori Mohan Ji, Maharaj Mahant Pt. Hariprasad Ji Piyari Sevayat, Ath shubh Samvat 2035 shak 1900* the last line cannot be read. Beside it is the symbolic representation in a marble arched circle having footprints, moon, *shankh*, *gada*, *surya*, flower, date plant.

## Rab Ji ka Ghera

"Sriji Mandir"

Rabji was in service of Bharatpur Maharaja. He had been granted land at Vrindaban. The full name of Rabji was Girdhari Saran Singh and was the relative of Rani Kishori. He constructed a temple dedicated to Radha Krishan. Architecturally it has no merit. The temple is constructed on a higher platform of the waist height, we reach there by steps. It is constructed of cream coloured stone. There is a verandah which is made up of square slabs of marble and red stone.

On entering the premises, on the right side, is a chamber used as the *rasoi*; smoke's blackness can still be seen. The peculiar feature is a well in another room at the side of rasoi. The food was taken to Thakurji by the flight of stairs which lead to the chamber in the temple enclosure. The left place may be for the watchman. At the side of the temple are two cubicals on opposite side perhaps used by the priests.

## Temple of Rani Kishori

On the road leading from Sonkh to Kumher lies a temple constructed by Rani Kishori. This temple is at a distance of about 8 kms. from Kumher Fort which can be seen from this place on a clear day.

It is the only temple which is constructed on an high elevation. Situated on a hillock, this temple is of plainer character but historically it is very important.[9] The gateway of the temple is built of red sandstone. Inside the temple which is enclosed by the wall, is a courtyard and two big rooms which are closed.[10] Towards the side

9. Folklore says that the temple is connected to the Kumher fort with an underground passage and Rani Kishori used to come to the temple from that way to worship.

10. Researcher could not see inside the rooms because Mahant did not permit him to do so.

of fort is the *Garbha Griha* in which the idols of Radha and Krishna can still be seen.

Standing atop the hillock one can see all around upto a very long distance, it is the ideal place of worship because of the peace and cool breeze which makes one to feel religious.

Further exacavation and inquiry is needed to explore the historicity of this temple and to know that if the underground passage actually exist.

### Temple at Gunsara

The temple at Gunsara constructed by Rani, the consort of Raja Randhir Singh, is situated in the garden which lies at the side of the tank. The group of monuments at Gunsara shows the ritualistic attitude of the rani as well as her love for nature.

The building is of much plainer architecture. In front of the temple is a courtyard in which stands a *khirni* and a *neem* tree. The front walls of the temple consists of five gates of which two are closed (probably later on).[11] The gates have multifoliated arch and petals, the peculiar artistic feature of Bharatpur State. The building is single storeyed.

In the varandah are two cubicles (Tibai) on either side. The *garbha griha* is next to the verandah which consists of the statue of Radha and Krishna. This temple of plainer character would have been of great importance during the reign of Raja Randhir Singh because this place was the dearest pleasure and worship resort of Rani Laxmi.

## Bharatpur Fort

### Idol of Hanumanji

This is situated in the Bharatpur Fort on high elevation. The idol built of black stone is situated on a circular platform. In it Hanumanji is seen carrying *Sanjivni Parbat* in his left hand and *gada* in the right. One of the foot of Hanumanji is on a rock on which an inscription in Sanskrit is engraved. Its translation in Hindi is given here.

---

11. These gates are filled with *Lakhori* bricks, rest of the temple is built of cream coloured stone.

As depicted from the inscription Hanumanji spent few moments on his way to battle field with *Sanjivni Parbat* remembering *Bharat* the brother of Ram. The idol was constructed in the reign of Bijendra Singh and the inscription itself is composed by some Bahadur Kavi of Chakotkat clan. The magnificant idol can be seen from every nook and corner of the Bharatpur city because of the high elevation and magnificance of the idol itself.

In his inscription, Bahadur Kavi seems to relate Ramayan episode to Bharatpur in order to give the capital of Jat *rajas* some religious importance.

**हनुमान प्रशस्त्रि**

जिस प्रकार समुद्र लहरों से युक्त अनेक नदियों के जलों को धारण करते हैं, उसी तरह से हनुमान जी भारी भारी पहाड़ों को धारण कर लेते हैं, प्राणियों के विघ्नों को पानी के बुलबुलों के समान शीघ्र नष्ट करते हैं ऐसे पराक्रमी हनुमान जी के लिए हम भक्ति से नमस्कार करते हैं।

संसार में राक्षसों के भय से पीड़ित मनुष्यों का उद्धार करने के लिए प्रसिद्ध है। भूत प्रेत पिशाच के संकट को नष्ट करने वाले अंजनी के पुत्र हनुमान की मंगल देने वाली सुंदर मूर्ति को श्रीमान बिजेंद्रसिंह ने स्थापित कराया।

रण में मूर्छित लक्ष्मणजी को जीवित करने के लिए संजीवनी औषधि को धारण करने वाले पहाड़ को बाएं हाथ में धारण करने वाले हनुमान आकाश में वेग के साथ उड़ते हुए राम के भाई भरत का स्मरण करते हुए, मैं मानता हूं कि वे इस भरतपुर नगर में कुछ क्षणों के लिए श्रद्धा पूर्वक ठहरें। वहीं हनुमानजी पहाड़ को धारण किए हुए गदा हाथ में लिए हुए, महान बलवान, मानों भरत का स्मरण करते हुए इस नगर में विराज मान हैं। विक्रम संवत 2000 में भरतपुर किले में मध्य इस मूर्ति की प्रतिष्ठा हुई है।

भरतपुर के राजा कृष्ण के भक्त विजेन्द्रसिंह के आदेश का परिपालन कर बहादुर कवि ने इस प्रशस्ति की रचना की है।

बहादुर कवि वीरदेवी माता के गर्भ से उत्पन्न हैं विष्णुदास के पुत्र हैं, चाकोतकर कुल में उत्पन्न हुए हैं।[12]

## Bihari Lal Ji Ka Mandir

12. Translated by Dr. Chandal Lal Parashar, former Head of the Sanskrit Deptt., K.M. Institute, Dr. B.R. Ambedkar University, Agra.

The temple lies at the side of Kishori Mahal. The gateway is elegantly carved. Passing through the corridor one could reach the courtyard. It is built of marble. On the left of the corridor is a verandah, it has five archs of which two at the corners are bow-shaped, three in th centre have multifoliated archs. In the verandah before the *garbha griha* are two idols of Hanumanji and Nag Baba (Garudji). It is the only maintained temple in the fort. On the right of the temple is the office of Rajasthan Ayurvedic Bhawan.

## (Bharatpur)

### Ganga Temple

It is the most imposing temple of the Bharatpur Kingdom. The foundation of the temple was laid by Raja Balwant Singh in 1845 A.D., This beautiful temple was constructed along with Jama Masjid at the instance of Balwant Singh out of contribution raised by the government servants, irrespective of their faith, who were then serving the state. Raja Balwant Singh ordered that Hindu and Muslim employees have to give their first salary according to their respective religions.[13] Where shall we find a better example of secular feeling, democratic practises, national outlook and liberal attitude in a period of narrow orthodoxy and fanaticism in the eighteenth and nineteenth century.

This temple built in cream coloured stone is two storeyed high. Climbing up a few stairs a slope leads to the entrance. It is a very rich and graceful composition. Every part of the temple is covered with the most delicate carving and is shaded above by broad eaves.

At the entrance there is an inscription which reads—

*Shri Gangya Namah*
*unto the pure all things are pure*
*In the year*
*1845 A.D. Samvat 1997*

Maharaja Balwant Singh ji Bahadur laid the foundation of this magnificant temple and consecrated it to his adored family deity Shri Ganga Maharani ji.

---

13. G.C. Dikshit, *Brajendra Vansh Bhaskar*, p. 182.

Its construction went on during the course of five generations of the ruling princes of the state at an enormous cost. In the reign of Maharaja Shri Brijendra Sawai Shri 108 Shri Brijendra Singh ji Sahib Bahadur, Bahadur Jung the installation ceremony of the deity was celebrated on the 22nd February 1937, (*Magh Shukla*) 12 *Chandravar Samvat* 1993.

The interior of the temple is markedly peristylar, and richly carved pillars are arranged so as to form hall and aisle. The inner walls of the hall are profusely carved. The roof of the temple is flat. The gateways are semi-circular and richly adorned.

The back of the temple is somewhat a tower like structure ornamented with flat bands and the whole tower surmounted by an *amalasila* or vase shaped stone. This tower has outlets of water beautifully built in the form of crocodile. Exquisite sculptures embellish the immense outer surface of this architectural masterpiece. The exterior of the tower is chiselled and moulded into figures of God. The sculptures, executed in cream coloured stone are small, delicate and full of the warmth of life. Ventilated outlet and doors also figures at the rear. Flat roof pillared hall and a structure consisting of a towered sanctum resembles the early period of Orissa temple architecture.

On the four corners of the temple are four pavilions which are somewhat of great architectural merit. Each pavilion is beautifully decorated with pillars and gateways with multifoliated arches. On either side of the gateway peculiar Bharatpur designs are carved. The pavilion is supported by the pillars which are carved above and below with incongruous animal figures and motifs, the roof is vaulted. The temple stands like a gem among the garland of monuments erected by the Bharatpur rajas.

## Mosque

### Jama Masjid

Situated in the midst of the city the mosque is built of cream coloured stone (probably the largest mosque of its kind) and was constructed at the instance of Maharaja Balwant Singh out of the contribution raised by the government servants who were than serving the state. He ordered Hindu-Muslim employees to give their first salary for the construction of the mosque and Ganga Mandir as stated earlier.

The mosque has a very big gateway with elegantly carved verses of Koran. It has a very big courtyard for saying prayers (*Namaj*).

The Jama Masjid throws light on the communal harmony of Jat rulers. This shows that the different religions were knotted into one and one could imagine the harmony with which the subjects lived in the Jat kingdom. It represent the emotional feeling of human heart which can eradicate the ill feeling, the greatest obstacle in creating communal harmony.

## *Chhattris*

Besides temples notable feature of Jat architecture are visible in the memorials found throughout the kingdom. Celebrated devotees commemorated by various types of shrines or memorials. The most common is a *Samadhi*, which may contain the ashes of a saint or some other relic. It is either a structure shaped like a round pointed cone or, more commonly, a marble slab carved with footprints and set into a raised platform, often with a dome or Kiosk (*chattri*) built over it. Venerations of memorials to the dead was, of course, an old tradition in India that was adapted to suit Hindu as well as Muslims.

## Maharaja Suraj Mal - *Chhattri* (Cenotaph) - Govardhan

A magnificient cenotaph was erected by Jawahar Singh in honour of his father, Suraj Mal, on the eastern bank of an artificial lake Kusum Sarovar which lies between Radha Kund and Govardhan. It is a hautingly beautiful example of Jat architecture.[14]

The Raja's monument is flanked on either side by two pavillions of some-what less dimension, commemorating his two queens Hansia and Kishori. The lofty terrace upon which they stand is 460 feet in length, with a long shallow pavilion serving as a screen at each end and nine two storied kiosks of varied outline to relieve the front.

The principal tomb is 57 feet square built of cream coloured and is of precisely the same style as the *chhattris* of Balwant Singh, Baldeo Singh and Randhir Singh. The best part of the design is the plinth which is at once bold in outline and delicate in finish with the

---

14. K. Natwar Singh, *Maharaja Suraj Mal*, p. 105.

curious blindness to practical requirements which appears to have characterised the Hindu architect are from the earliest period to the present, the decorated panels have been continued all round the four sides of the building without a blank space being left anywhere for the steps which the height from the ground renders absolute necessary.[15]

The architecture and carving of the square chamber is in the best pierced stone style with vaulted ceiling. The interior of the *chhattri* is specially fine. The crescent shaped space in ceiling on the broad frieze (just below the dome) on each wall is executed with a beautiful fresco depicting a scene in the life of Suraj Mal and giving a vivid picture of the dress, weapons, architecture etc. of those times and an idea of the splendour of Indian raja's court. The frescro painting on the west depicts a darbar assembly probably at Deeg, on the north depicts a royal procession with the raja seated on an elephant and accompanied of camels, elephants, horses (all full caparisoned). The next picture shows Suraj Mal arriving in state with his courtiers for Dushera puja; and the next shows his hunting grounds (which lay between Bharatpur and Deeg) describing a variety of the hunt; figurines (in the round) of a variety of musicians ornament the base of the pendentives which are richly ornamented.

The arches are thoroughly naturalized, the details are also in the main dictated by Mughal precedent but they are carried out with much of the Hindu solidity and exuberance of fanciful decoration. The moulding are shallower and the wall ornamentation consists of nothing but an endless succession of 'niches' and 'vases' repeated with wearisome uniformity.

The Bangla or oblong alcove with a vaulted roof of curvilinear outline is a prominent feature of the cenotaph and is introduced into some parts of every facade. From the name it may be inferred that it was borrowed from Bengal and was probably intended as a copy of the ordinary cottage roof made of bent bamboos. It does not appear in upper India till the reign of Aurangzeb; the earliest example in the region is in Mathura, being the alcoves of the mosque built by Abd-un-Nabi in 1661 A.D.

This *chhattri* flanked with three others are very elegantly grouped piles of building and have an extremely picturesque effect

15. F.S. Growse, *Mathura : A District Memoir*, pp. 306-07.

which is heightened by the *sarovar* in front of them.

In the main chamber there is a marble slab embedded in the middle of the floor on which are carved symbolic representation.

The painting in the ceiling indicates the then prevailing condition in the Jat kingdom. In villages, as the chattri of Suraj Mal painting directs, dancing and folk music formed the chief entertainments. Meos were also very much efficient in throwing javelins, as the 'chhattri' painting indicates, Maharaja Suraj Mal standing and a Meo throwing Javelins. The wielding clubs and play of swords and use of dumb bells were very common. *Ekkas* and *Raths* as indicated by the chhattri were common vehicles used for travelling by civilians. Camels and horses were confined to the rich and the poor walked on foot.

On the right side of the principal tomb is the *chhattri* of Maharani Kishori.[16] The cenotaph is somewhat lesser in dimension. It stands on the double cloistered coloumns. The striking feature of this cenotaph is the mural paintings at the roof and at the walls.

On the right side is a mural painting in which Lord Krishna is seen holding the Govardhan Parvat on his finger. Lord Krishna is supported by his brother Balaram and gopies. Beneath the parvat can be seen people, with their belongings, cattles and even birds taking shelter. Childrens are also seen playing on top of the hill probably God Indra can be seen.

Another painting depicts the scene of Rani Kishori's marriage with Raja Suraj Mal. On this occasion people are playing trumpets and *Torahi*, all gods and goddesses are seen in the painting blessing the newly wedded couple and the pandit is seen chanting hyms. On the roof women are seen singing songs on the auspicious occasion of the marriage. This mural painting probably indicates the grand ceremony that took place on this occasion.

The third painting depicts a war scene. It shows war between two armies, soldiers on foot, horsemen and elephant riders fighting each other. Soldiers can be seen lying slayed on the ground. The use of arrows is easily depicted. A woman is standing on the gate of the fort commanding the army from inside. In the battlefield a chariot can also be seen which carries the king and queen. On the top of the door can be seen an image of a god. On the upper floor three women

16. Fransoo, *Tawarikh-i-Hunud*, 22a-22b.

are standing which may be the other queens of Raja Suraj Mal. Besides showing the masculine deeds of the queen the painting shows that the use of bow and arrow, swords and archers were the common mode of warfare. It also indicates that Jat women played active role in the time of danger. Many historians have praised the valour of Jat women in the battle field.[17] At the time of crisis, they preferred to die fighting unlike the Rajput women.[18] They fought shoulder to shoulder with their husbands.[19]

Though the tomb is a part of Suraj Mal's chhattri and by itself is of no architectural merit, yet, it shows the love of the Raja towards Rani Kishori, her place in the kingdom and above all the

---

17. Khair-ud-din Muhammad Allahabadi, *The Ibratnama*, (Ms) says "No 'Johar seemed to have been lighted at Deeg; women and children were put to the sword.", cited by Qanungo, *History of the Jats*, p. 174.
18. Le Nabob Rene Madec, Sec. 48; He notices that three wives of Nawal Singh prayed to the palace-eunuch to kill them after the capture of the city by Najaf Khan. "They lay on the carpet and he cut off the heads of all the three of them one after another and ended by killing himself on the corpses."
19. *Storio do Mogor*, tr. by W. Irvine, Vol. I, P. 134; it reads that "There is nothing unusual in the slaughter of females by the Jats at Deeg." Speaking of the Jats in the reign of Akbar, Manucci says "In order to defend themselves these villagers hid in thorny shurbs or retired behind the slight walls surrounding their villages. The women stood behind their husbands with spears and arrows. When the husband had shot off his matchlock his wife handed him the lance while she reloaded the matchlock. Thus did they defend themselves until they were no longer able to continue. When reduced to extremity, they cut their wives' and daughters' throats and then in desperation they threw themselves against the enemy's ranks and several times they succeeded in gaining the day by mere reckless courage."

paintings depict prevailing conditions, religious beliefs and mode of warfare. Rani Kishori rightly deserves the place at the side of her husband because her genius and resourcefulness saved the fortunes of Bharatpur many a time from almost inevitable ruin.

On the left side of the principal tomb is the chhattri of Maharani Hansia. She was the consort of Maharaja Suraj Mal. She was the daughter of Chowdhari Rati Ram Jat of Salempur.[20] It lies opposite the cenotaph of Rani Kishori. The striking feature of this monument of lesser dimension is the mural paintings at the roof and at the wall.

The painting in the interior of the bow-shaped roof is a bit heavy and tasteless as Hindu attempts at pictorial art generally are.[21] The mural painting on the side wall depicts the queen Hansia and Maharaja swinging in a swing tied to a tree with the help of ropes, maybe the scene of monsoon. Two maid servants are swinging it while the third is playing on the *dholak*, a peacock is sitting and admiring the love play of the king and queen. This romantic painting shows that Suraj Mal loved Hansia the most. The location of the cenotaph also confirms my view. The painting is defective since an extra line is seen around the king and the queen.

Another painting shows the scene of the palace. The King is entering the palace, his horse can also be seen. On the first floor, servants are playing trumpets signalling the arrival of the king. On the next floor Brahmins are chanting the hymes and the king is receiving blessings from the incarnations of god. The Rani is sitting in a balcony and the maid servants all around are singing and dancing. The painting is probably depicting some auspicious occasion on which a grand feast is celebrated while at the top fairies are admiring and dancing.

Another mural painting depicts the scene of a river which is probably Jamuna. The painting indicates the occasion of some festival, probably *Janamashtmi*, because a scene shows Vasudev carrying the

---

20. Fransoo, *Tarikh-i-Hunud*, 22a-22b.
21. F.S. Growse, *Mathura : A District Memoir*, p. 307.

infant Lord Krishna and Sheshnag protecting the two. Raja is seen sailing down the river in a boat. At the rear *ghat* is seen people bathing and Brahmins chanting hymns. This shows the grandeur with which festivals were celebrated in the kingdom. The traditional glory of *Janamashtmi* started by Bharatpur ruler is still maintained in Govardhan and Mathura.

Though the monument is not of any architectural merit and to say more is a small part of the magnificant *chhattri* but the mural paintings show the everyday life, festivities and other grand occassions held in those days. Again the monument shows the closeness which the Rani had with Maharaja Suraj Mal.

Besides the tomb of Hansia is another tomb which may probably belong to some faithful maid servant of the queen. But only the tomb of Rani Hansia has symbolic representations of Bharatpur State.

The cenotaphs of Hansia and Kishori show their reputation, love, affection and closeness which they had with Maharaja Suraj Mal who loved them most beside having more than six wives.

## *Chhattri* of Raja Jawahar Singh

On the north side of Maharaja Suraj Mal's cenotaph lies the unfinished *chhattri* of Raja Jawahar Singh, probably the work was interrupted by Muslim inroad and it was never renewed.[22]

At present the unfinished cenotaph is almost in ruins. The place is surrounded all about by *babul* trees. Only the platform and a pathway is seen. The platform built of cream coloured stone is square in shape. There are signs which show that further construction was probably bound to be done. The platform is attached to a long pathway built of red and cream coloured stones. Nothing else can be traced from the cenotaph of such mighty and worthy successor of Maharaja Suraj Mal. It is painful to see the ruined cenotaph of a ruler whose love of art and architecture can be seen from the edifices which were renovated or constructed at his instance.

## *Chhattri* of Raja Ratan Singh at Vrindaban

Near the temple of Madan Mohan Ji is an unfinished *Chhattri* belonging to Ratan Singh. It is in the same state as it was left at the

22. F.S. Growse, *Mathura : A District Memoir*, p. 308.

time of his death. The place at present is a dirty gallery and still known by the name of Ratan *Chhattri*.

Ratan Singh was the immediate successor of Raja Jawahar Singh. Ratan Singh would have inherited his father Suraj Mal and mother Ganga's[23] architectural inclination for he had commenced what promised to a very large and handsome mausoleum for the reception of his own funeral ashes but died before the work had advanced beyond the first storey.[24]

The cenotaph was probably planned square in shape. The main entrance, now blocked by illegal occupation has six gates with multifoliated arches. The whole structure is composed of cream coloured stone.

Nothing of architectural merit is left besides the plinth which once beared the funeral ashes of the most romantic king of Bharatpur state. The plinth is of waist height, beautifully carved and built of cream coloured stone. One can reach the plinth by climbing the stairs from either side of the building. Unfinished and now ruined cubicals are seen on all the four sides. At present this *chabutra* is covered all around by *kandas* (cow dung). The cenotaph is in such a dilapidated state that one has to pass from dirt and filth before reaching the forgotten monument.

---

23. Ganga Rani, the consort of Suraj Mal hailed from a village Bichawindi. She is credited with Ganga Mohan Kunj at Vrindaban.
24. F.S. Growse, *Mathura : A District Memoir*, p. 41, footnote.

35. Front view, Ganga temple, Bharatpur

36. Rear view, Ganga temple

37. Decorated pillar at Ganga temple

38. Engraved wall, Ganga temple

39. A view of Jama Masjid from Bharatpur fort

40. Multifoliated (cusped) arch, Ganga Mandir

41. Idol of Hanumanji, Bharatpur fort

42. Outlet in the form of crocodile, Ganga Mandir

43. Temple of Rani Kishori on the outskirts of Kumher

44. Temple at Gunsara

45. *Chhattri* of Rani Kishori, Govardhan

46. *Chhattri* of Maharaja Suraj Mal at Kusum Sarovar Govardhan

47. Ruined mural paintings depicting the Ras Leela
cenotaph of Suraj Mal

48. Ruined plinth, cenotaph of Maharaja Suraj Mal

49. Side view - Suraj Mal *Chhattri*

50. Mural painting at the roof (cenotaph of Suraj Mal)

51. One of the doors of the principal chamber (cenotaph of Suraj Mal)

52. Marble slab where the tooth of Suraj Mal is buried marked with symbolic representation

53. Mural painting depicting the Durbar scene
(cenotaph of Suraj Mal)

54. Mural painting at the roof
(cenotaph of Suraj Mal)

55. Mural paintings on the wall
(*Chhattri* of Suraj Mal)

56. Mural painting on the side of the roof
(Cenotaph of Suraj Mal)

57. Mural painting depicting the marriage ceremony *Chhattri* of Rani Kishori - Cenotaph Maharaja Suraj Mal

58. Mural painting depicting Lord Krishna holding Govardhan Parvat - *Chhattri* of Rani Kishori

59. Mural painting depicting the war scene (*Chhattri* Rani Kishori)

60. Mural painting on the wall (*Chhattri* Rani Kishori)

61. Suraj Mal and Rani Hansia swinging *Chhattri*
Rani Hansia -Cenotaph of Suraj Mal

62. Mural painting at the roof (*Chhattri* of Rani Hansia)

63. Mural painting depicting the scene of the palace
(*Chhattri* Rani Hansia)

64. River scene - *Chhattri* Rani Hansia

65. Ruined plinth, Cenotaph of Jawahar Singh (Govardhan)

66. Incomplete structure, Cenotaph of Jawahar Singh

## *Chhattri* of Raja Baldeo Singh

On the opposite side of Manasi Ganga there is a group of three stately cenotaphs in memory of Raja Baldeo Singh, Balwant Singh and Randhir Singh respectively. Among them the largest and most delicate cenotaph belongs to Baldeo Singh. Though all of them are somewhat of similar design but they differ in size and the mural paintings adorned on them. All these chhattri's are very elegantly grouped and have an extremely picturesque effect, which is heightened by the *panch tirth* tank in front of them.[25]

The cenotaph consists of a substantial and lofty square masonry terrace with corner kiosks and lateral alcoves. The monument is at the centre which is further raised on a richly decorated plinth. The underground room is enclosed in a colonnade of five open arches on each side. It is a square apartment surmounted by a dome and having each wall divided into three sections, of which one is left for the doorway and the remainder are filled in with reticulated tracery. The cloister has a small dome on every side and the curious curvilinear roof, distinctive of the style, over the central compartments.

The *chhattri* is adorned with beautiful doors having multifoliated arches. The panels of the door is striking too. The interior of the cenotaph is also as fascinating and remarkable as the exterior one, if not more on account of pietra dura, mural paintings, inlay work on the roof, cenotaph and the screen surrounding the cenotaph.

They generate among the viewers a feeling of admiration for the masters of this monuments who lived in the days gone by.[26] In the centre of this structure lies the receptacles which hold the remains of Baldeo Singh. The marble slab which contains the symbolic representations viz. foot marks, dragger, sword, bead, *gada* and *shankh*. This slab is adorned by pietra dura on all sides. It shows floral design in reddish cornelian, yellow jasper, blacks onyx and agate and embossed floral design.

---

25. F.S. Growse, *Mathura : A District Memoir*, p. 307.
26. It is wrong on the part of great scholar like F.S. Growse to describe it as a monument of no great merit and to say that they were executed by a contractor who scamped the work to increase his own profit. He writes "The decorative details are mostly poor in themselves and are repeated with a monotonous uniformity which contrasts most disagreeably with the rich variety of design that distinguishes all the more important buildings either in Mathura or Vrindaban. The paintings on the interior of the domes is also as heavy and tasteless as Hindu generally attempts at pictorial art." (F.S. Growse, *Mathura : A District Memoir*, p. 307.)

Being comparatively an extensive style of architectural decoration, the art of pietra dura was not in common practice among the Jat rulers. Even in India, the art was not uncommon before it was embellished on Baldeo Singh's cenotaph. The roof of the central room which contains the ashes of Baldeo Singh is decorated with paintings in miniature with scenes from the life of Lord Krishna. The roof adorned with glass work is slowly withering away with the time.

Another striking aspect of the monument are the *jali* work all around the central room and the hexagon shaped stairs supported on the stone piece.

This memorable cenotaph of Baldeo Singh, who died in 1825, was erected by his son and successor, the late Raja Balwant Singh, who was placed on the throne after the reduction of the fort of Bharatpur by Lord Combermere in 1826.

## ***Chhattri* of Raja Balwant Singh**

The cenotaph is somewhat smaller than that of Balwant Singh's father Baldeo Singh. It consists of a lofty and substantial square masonry terrace with lateral alcoves and corner kiosks. The centre is raised on a rich decorated plinth. The cella, enclosed in a colonnade of five open arches on each side, is a square apartment surmounted by a dome and having each wall divided into three bays of which one is left for the door way and the rest are filled in with reticulated decorative pattern in stone work.

In the centre of the *chhattri* lies the slab which holds the remains of Balwant Singh. The slab consists of symbolic representation which is the peculiar feature of a Jat raja's cenotaph. The main attraction of the viewers are the mural paintings which depicts the life history of Raja Balwant Singh. In one of the paintings Raja Balwant Singh as a child is seen with an English gentleman, perhaps the British regent of the Raja. This painting shows the meeting of the infant Raja with Englishman after the successful assault of Britishers on the Lohagarh fort.[27] In another picture Raja Balwant Singh is seen sitting on the royal throne in his manhood. The use of blue, black, red, golden and green colour is clearly seen in the paintings. The roof of the central dome is also beautifully painted, which further heightened the beauty of the monument. The British

27. Rao Durjan Sal who was the regent and the uncle of the infant ruler, Balwant Singh, illegally occupied the throne. Lord Combermere attacked the Bharatpur Fort to help Balwant Singh the rightful heir of throne to obtain his legal right.

army figures conspicuously in the paintings on the ceilings of the pavilions.

## *Chhattri* of Raja Randhir Singh

The *chhattri* of Raja Randhir Singh is of similar design as the *chhattries* of Raja Baldeo Singh and Raja Balwant Singh. The plan executed in the construction is also the same. Corner kiosks and lateral alcoves in the centre, the underground room in a colonnade of fine open arches, a square apartment surmounted by a dome is more or less the same in design except the size. The cloister has a small dome at each corner and the curvilinear roof over the central compartments.

## Burial Ground

Along the boundary of *chhattries* of Raja Baldeo Singh and Balwant Singh is the cemetery of Bharatpur Rajas. It contains small brick structures commemorating the later Bharatpur Rajas and their family members receptacles. It includes the cenotaph of Raja Ram Singh,[28] Maharaja Kishan Singh,[29] wife of Raja Kishan Singh etc.

In 1803 Govardhan was granted free of assessment to Kunwar Lachhman Singh, the youngest son of Raja Ranjit Singh of Bharatpur, but on his death in 1826 it was resumed by the government and annexed to the district of Agra. Now it is in the Mathura District.

Britain was repeatedly solicited by Bharatpur Raja to cede Govardhan to him in exchange for another territory of equal value. It contains so many memorials of the ancestors of the Jats of Bharatpur that the request was very natural one. After independence the cenotaphs remained the private property of the Bharatpur Raja but are poorly looked after.[30]

---

28. Raja Ram Singh is credited of the construction of Bund Baretha.
29. Maharaja Kishan Singh erected Vasant Bhawan at Bund Baretha.
30. There are merely two servants to look after the monuments. One out of them, Ramesh Chandra works for 24 hours on the wages of 300 per month. They are hereditary keepers, his father, Ballo Ram, was also the keeper. According to him four keepers are allotted but only two work here.

67. Pathway, *Chhattri* of Jawahar Singh

68. Spikes at the tomb (Govardhan)

69. Plinth, *Chhattri* of Raja Ratan Singh, Brindaban

70. Ruined and incomplete front, Cenotaph of Ratan Singh

71. *Chhattri* of Raja Baldeo Singh - Govardhan

72. Principal tomb with decorated stairs
(*Chhattri* Raja Baldeo Singh)

73. Decorated pillar and Jali work
(*Chhattri* of Raja Baldeo Singh)

74. Broken Jalis (*Chhattri* of Raja Baldeo Singh)

75. Glass work with idols of Lord Krishna
(roof of Raja Baldeo Singh's Cenotaph)

76. Pietra Dura on the principal grave
(*Chhattri* of Raja Baldeo Singh)

77. Kiosks and the view of the *Chhattri* of Raja Balwant Singh (Govardhan)

78. Mural painting at the roof (Cenotaph Raja Baldeo Singh)

79. Mural painting depicting Raja Balwant Singh sitting on the throne

80. Faded mural painting depicting infant Raja Balwant Singh with the British officer (Regent)

81. Side view of Raja Baldeo Singh's Cenotaph

82. *Chhattri* of Raja Randhir Singh

83. Decorated stairs of Raja Baldeo Singh
(in the rear is the Cenotaph of Raja Randhir Singh)

84. Burial ground of Bharatpur rulers (Govardhan)

## *Chapter 8*

# Conclusion

A comprehensive survey of the Jat monuments spread throughout the erstwhile Bharatpur kingdom reveals not only a peculiar beauty of style and execution but also specific features and techniques which throw ample light on the character and personality of the rulers and their administration. Constructing a methodological frame work and analysing the source material are vital to my topic.

The boundaries of the Bharatpur State encompass one of the best cultural traditions of India, the antiquity of which can be traced to very ancient times. Jats by nature were strong yet peace loving race with a legacy of democratic traditions. Changes in agrarian relations and excesses of the centralized despotic regime of Delhi forced them to unite for their rights. The jagir system of the Mughals increased the exploitation of Jat peasantry. After various local uprisings under local chieftains, the emergence of Thakur Badan Singh was a watershed in Jat history. Inclining towards the sovereign power, he combined coercion with conciliation and carved out the Jat State of Bharatpur. It was left for Suraj Mal to establish the glory and grandeur of the Jats. This tradition was continued by his successors.

Leafing through the history of Jat rulers upto the amalgamation of the Jat State in the Indian Union one can visualize the transformation of the militant agriculturist crusaders into founders of a stable politico-economic structure and great builders. Their political apparatus, social customs, clan structure are all visible in the monuments they have bequeathed to posterity. Through fieldwork and a scientific study of the monuments it is clear that the geographical situation also played a significant role in the construction of these monuments. The consorts of the rulers too erected beautiful buildings at religious places near their state. What we call the Jat style of architecture is represented mainly by the forts, mansion, cenotaphs and other religious and secular buildings. Formality, balance and symmetry are the essentials of this architecture.

Badan Singh and his two sons, Suraj Mal and Pratap Singh are credited to have built the most number of Jat monuments. The big and invincible forts of Bharatpur, Deeg, Wair and Kumher clearly reflect the military talents of Raja Suraj Mal and with it the statesmanship and strategical wisdom of Badan Singh. These forts were constructed at places advised by Badan Singh while the construction was laid according to the imagination of Raja Suraj Mal. The beautiful gardens at Wair which still exist in a dilapidated state show the love of nature and poetic feeling of Pratap Singh, the younger brother of Suraj Mal. The palaces at Deeg show the grandeur and leisure loving nature of Raja Badan Singh. There are numerous palaces erected in the holy city of Vrindaban by various queens. Rani Kishori, Rani Ganga and Rani Laxmi are few among them who constructed very beautiful palaces in the kingdom.

Besides being courageous and good statesmen, the Jat rulers were also religious by nature. Raja Badan Singh erected a temple known by the poetic name of Dhir Samir. He decided to make Deeg his capital on the advice of a holy man named, Pritam Das. In the same way Suraj Mal was advised by a Naga saint to build a fort at the site of demolished Fateh-garhi of Sogharias. On the occasion of Deepawali the ceremony of Deep Dan which was started by Suraj Mal in Govardhan is still observed. His son, Jawahar Singh, constructed and renovated the temples at Wati (Mathura), Shahpur (near Deeg), and Deeg town. He also got a *ghat* built at Pushkar lake, the famous Hindu place of pilgrimage, and opened it for the common use of all communities and creeds. A priest was appointed to look after and manage them and his salary was paid by the Bharatpur State. It is interesting to note that this office of the priest continued uninterrupted till the merger of the princely states with India. Where shall we find a better example of secular feeling, democratic practices, national outlook and liberal attitude in a period of narrow orthodoxy and fanaticism of the eighteenth century? His successors continued to erect temple, mosques and *ghats* which reflect the religious nature and religious tolerance of the Jat rulers.

Another striking aspect of the Jat rulers was the love and respect they showed towards their parents. This attitude of them make them unparallel in medieval Indian history. Raja Suraj Mal ruled not less than twenty years in the name of Badan Singh. Throughout this period he remained as an obedient son. He fulfilled all the desires of his father. He also fulfilled his dream by turning the sleepy town of Deeg into capital studded with exquisite palaces and invincible fort. His son, Jawahar Singh, revolted against him because of his ambitions but soon realised his mistake. After his father's death he put his life at stake to avenge the death of his father. His affection and love for his father is reflected from the magnificent cenotaph he constructed at Govardhan to commemorate him. Cenotaphs of Randhir Singh, Baldev Singh and Raja Balwant Singh add another feather to the cap of affection shown by the Jat rulers.

The Jat rulers were generous towards their subjects. The construction of dams, *sarais* (inns), *baolis* (step wells) shows their love and affection they had for their subjects. For the security of their own authority. The Jata also built forts in tune with times at Bharatpur, Deeg, Kumher, Wair, Aring, Thun, Sonkh, Badan Garhi, Laher and other places.

Sufficient information exists about the technique of raising forts of various types and categories in the Vedic, Puranic and classical literature of India. The science of forts and fortifications in medieavel period was so advanced that the shilpasāśtras describe not less than 19 forms of forts with vivid defensive scheme.

The Bharatpur fort, also named as Lohagaıh, was the most formidable fort of the Jats. Its construction, broad moat, and position are the factors responsible for the invincibility of the fort. The entire region surrounding the fort is a low lying land which has very little capacity to absorb water and which becomes a marshy land in the rainy season. The suitable geography of this region has provided natural strength for defensive devices. Harsh and hot-saline and oily contents of water renders it unfit for drinking. The sub tropical climate also provides natural calamity for the besiegers. Emphasis is laid on the factors responsible for the impregnability of the fort apart from the natural factor.

The planning and architecture of the forts, specially, of Bharatpur, Deeg, Kumher and Wair reveal the wonderful creativity of the indigenous techniques of the Jats. The mud rampart, probably the city wall, surrounds the main fort at a distance of two to three kos followed by *marhalas* at a distance of one *kos*. The inner wall surrounding or encircling the fort is very solid. These mud ramparts coated with bricks and rocks were incredibly formidable in dimension. These two mud walls are intervened by abroad moat (the fort of Kumher is an exception) which were always kept filled with water and ferocious aquatics were tamed in them. The Jat rulers prepared a threefold line of defence. The fort and the city was prepared in such a way that the canon shell could not damage either of the two. The entrance gate of the forts were also covered with spiked metal which further strengthened the defence of the fort. The Jat forts are studded with the bastions on which were mounted the huge guns. The top of the towers and gate is also crowned with parapet and embrasures. The very high perpendicular and steep towers provided no opportunity for escalading.

Another characteristic of Jat forts is the regular supply of water. For maintaining potable supply of water a number of wells were dug inside the fort which were kept under tight security. The water was drawn out with the help of the bullocks. But except the Lohagarh and Wair Forts, rest of the Jat forts are not so large as to accomodate much army and space for storage of food stuffs. Our study systematically provides the topography, construction, merits and demerits of the Jat forts and tries to explain that why they were regarded unique in India from the point of view of toughness, durability and accessibility.

Apart from the extensive study of the forts and fortifications, the researcher also surveyed other monuments erected inside the fort. These monuments, like administrative buildings, palaces, gardens, water supply system, temples and other miscellaneous structures are elaborately dealt with under subsequent chapters. For security, the palaces of the Jat rulers, specially in the Bharatpur and Deeg forts, are situated in the centre. These palaces, are spacious and double storeyed with bow shaped roofs and elegant balconies representing Mughal architecture.

Another striking characteristic of the Bharatpur Fort is the temple of Lord Krishna erected in simple style under the different names such as Gopalji, Man Mohanji, Chaturbhuj and Raghunathji. No other fort in India has temples dedicated to Lord Krishna.

The palace architecture of the Jat rulers of Bharatpur maybe divided broadly into two groups. The first group consisting of high class houses which were generally double storeyed *Dumanjila*. They were built around *chowks* with stone and brick walls, tile roofs and verandahs. The second group consists of the most charismatic of the Jat structures, the palaces at Deeg. Their sophistication, symmetrical order, delicate carvings and the immaculate roofing pattern attract the attention of the viewers. Other characteristics include massive structures, internal arrangements and simpler plastic decorations in brackets and pillars. Primarily of trabeate order, the Jat style uses engrailed arches resting on ornate pillars, flat roof terraces, balconies and pavillions with Bengal roof, Hypostylar halls, double eaves, spacious internal arrangements and moderate structural height. Other attractions include pillars with floral bases, protecting dripstones and tapering shafts. Variety of arches are used including semi circular, trefoil and pointed apses. A harmonious relationship exists between the architecture and the garden plan.

Gardens, tanks, dams and *ghats* constructed by the rulers of Bharatpur are exquisite examples of the architectural legacy of the Jats. The history of the gardens can be traced systematically from the time of Indo-Aryans. A number of categories of the gardens have been discussed by Vatsyayāna such as *pramododyānā*, *udyāna*, *vṛksharāṭikā* for kings, queens and ministers and *Nandanavana* dedicated to Lord Indra. The geometric pattern on which the Bharatpur State gardens are laid was considered to be the best for town planning in ancient times. The Jat art of gardening has been evaluated by a comparison of the data related with the art of gardening of the Mughals and Rajputs. The layout of the Jat garden at Deeg is based on the Mughal horticulture plan called *chār-bāgh*. The notable significance of these gardens is their sunken appearance.

The Jat architects achieved great success in producing artificial charms of water and monsoonal feeling during excessive heat than any one else. Besides the canals and tanks, the major medium of water display, are chutes fountains, cascades and the system of initiating beauties of the monsoon. The last system is decidedly and originally Indian in character. The Jat rulers specially, Badan Singh and Suraj Mal, are credited to introduce the system of enjoying beauties of the monsoon rains and achieved perfection in creating artificial charm by combining the gardens with the romantic lakes and enjoying the artificial monsoon rain even in extreme heat. The ornate stone flower beds in the gardens of Wair resembles the stone parterres in Amber gardens based upon the star which was held in special esteem by the Seljuk Turks and makes one believe that the immigrants of Turkish origin had at one time taken refuge in Rajputana.

About the flora grown at Deeg gardens nothing of special note can be said but the striking aspect of other gardens in Braj region, at Wair and Bharatpur is the common presence of *Khirni* trees. Besides it the gardens are full of *Pilu* or Salvadore Obeoides trees which are very old with hollow trunks and strangely distorted and gnarled branches.

The Jat rulers constructed many *pākkā tālābs*, few were constructed from religious point of view, others for entertainment, to supply water to the gardens and for the use of public welfare. The tanks at Deeg, Gunsara, Govardhan and Agra are described in detail. Few of the tanks such as *Panch Tirth Kund* and Tank at Parsoli derive their origin from the time of Lord Krishna. They are regarded as holy tanks and till present are the centre of pilgrims.

The Jat rulers also constructed dams for proper water supply to their forts and palaces as well as for the public welfare. The pioneer dam amongst hundreds constructed by them is Bund Baretha which is still active and serves Bharatpur city till today. Bund Baretha was constructed in two phases, the purpose being to regulate the water supply of river Kakunda and to employ more than 3,000 people at the time of drought. A detailed description regarding the technical aspect of the dam includes the table which shows the reduced level contours, spread bighas, capacity per cubic feet and the flood level from the time of its construction.

The construction of the *ghats* on the river banks is a peculiar feature of Indian architecture. The aim of constructing these *ghats* was to afford easy access to bathers by the flight of slabs leading to the river. Besides the religious and cultural significance, the *ghats* prevented the soil erosion which could have threatened human lives. Besides the history, importance and architecture of the *ghats*, matter of concern is the deplorable condition in which they are at present.

The state of temples built by the Jat rulers is however much better. They reflect the devotion and dedication of not only the Jat ruling family but also of the contemporary society. They continued the traditions of the established conventions of the buildings. Important temples include Nand Baba at Nand Gaon, Kishori Mohan temple of Vrindaban, temple at Gunsara, Behari Lalji Ka Mandir and Hanuman Mandir at Bharatpur fort and above all Ganga temple and Laxman temple also Jama Masjid at Bharatpur.

Memorials in the form of *chhattris* abound in the Jat Kingdom. They include that of Suraj Mal, Jawahar Singh, Baldeo Singh, Balwant Singh and Randhir Singh at Govardhan. An important burial ground of the ruling family is also at Govardhan. The chief characteristic of these *chhattris* are the mural paintings on the walls and the roof. The pictures depict the then prevailing condition in the Bharatpur State. It shows the princely grandeur, festivals at royal palaces, mode of warfare and festive scenes. They also show the common vehicles used and the subjects love for adventurous games.

Thus we can see that the Jat kingdom of Bharatpur has bequeathed to posterity a distinct tradition of architecture. It saw its fruition in the reign of Badan Singh and Suraj Mal. It is not only the embodiment of the visions of the Jat rulers but also the culmination of a process of cultural mobility which was an important part of Braj region. It is a valuable contribution to the stream of Indian culture and civilization. It is unfortunate that the post independence era saw the decline of this wonderful tradition. The Bharatpur royal house does not keep systematic records of their monuments. Gradually the property comprising the precious monuments are either sold by or are illegally occupied. Members of the royal house should come forward to protect their ancestral invaluable tradition. It must be admitted that the traditional Bharatpur frontier is very wide and it is greatly in need of rectification. Its continuity is not the order of the day and conservation and preservation of these immaculate structures is a requirement. A heritage conservation zone should immediately be established with its nucleus at Deeg.

# Bibliography


**I. Original Sources**

***A. Persian***

1. *Bayan-i-Waqai* by Adbul Karim Kashmiri.
2. *Imad-us-Saadat* by Ghulam Ali Naqvi. Jamia Milia Library.
3. *Maasir-i-Alamgiri* by Muhammad Saqi Mustaid Khan. Bibiography, Index, Serial Calcutta.
4. *Siyar-ul-Mutakherin* by Ghulam Husain Khan Tabatabai. It was written in 1780 A.D. and was translated by Raymond or Haji Mustafa. Reprinted in 4 volumes from Calcutta 1902, Siyar covers in its narrative a long range of the Jat history.
5. *Tawarikh-i-Hunud* by Frans Gottlieb Kuen, pen named Fransoo (1777 to 1861). He was a German native of Poland, migrating to India and serving under captain Samru. The manuscript written in persian for presentation to captain Abraham Lockett, is the most valuable account of the Bharatpur Rajas upto 1826 A.D. based on the Hindu sources and the information derived from the persian munshis of the Bharatpur court.
6. *Shahnama Munawwar Kalam* by Shivdas Lakhanavi, translated by Askari, Patna, 1968

***B. French***

1. Wendel's *Memoirs on the Origin, Growth and Present State of Jat Power in Hindustan (1768)* English edition (1991), edited and annotated by Jean Deloche. He was in the service of Maharaja Jawahar Singh of Bharatpur. He stayed at Agra from 1751 until his death in 1803 A.D. He supplied secret informations to the English especially about the Jats.
2. Le Journal Du Voyage du Bengale a Delby (Paris Ms.) by L.L. Dolisy De Modave. Extracts of this eye witness account have been translated by Jadu Nath Sarkar entitled, 'The Delhi Empire A Century After Bernier, in Islamic culture XI, 1937.

3. *Storia Do Mogor* by Niccolao Manucci. Translated by William Irvine, vols. I (1906), III (1907), London, II (1966), Calcutta.

***C. Hindi***

1. *Somnath Granthawali* by Somnath the great grandson of Narottam Mishra, who hailed from Mathura. He enjoyed the patronage of Suraj Mal for some time and then lived at the court of Suraj Mal's brother Pratap Singh and nephew, Bahadur Singh at Wair. *Somnath Granthawali* is the collection of his works published by Kashi Nagari Pracharini Sabha. It is edited by Sudhakar Pande, Kashi, 1971. The work includes *Ras Peeushnidhi* (pp. 1-224), *Madhav Vinod* (pp. 317-498), *Ras Panchadhai* and *Shrinagar Vilas*. The *Ras Peeushnidhi* (pp. 2-8) and *Madhav Vinod* (pp. 317-20) generally follow the contents of *Dirgha Nagar Varnan*. this Hindi Ms. is the only work having any historical value. The Ms. runs into seven pages and ends abruptly. It describes the lay out of Deeg palaces and throw light on the construction and supplied material.
2. *Sujan Charitra* by Sudan. Written in 1754, Ist edition Kashi. It gives an account of the exploits of Suraj Mal from 1745, to the beginning of 1754. Sudan, a native of Mathura and a close companion of Suraj Mal, had access to information not available to outsiders.

**II. Secondary Sources**

***General***

**1. English**

Acharya, P.K.: *Encyclopaedia of Hindu Architecture*, Delhi, 1978.

Aitchison, C.U.: *A collection of treaties, engagements and Sanads*, Vol. III.

Ali, R.: Islamic Architecture in India after Independence, Pune, 1978, Vol. XXXVII.

Bhargava, M.L.: *A Geography of Rig Vedic India*, Lucknow, 1964.

Creighton, J.N.: *The Narrative of the Siege and Capture of Bharatpur*, Published at London, 1830.

Datta, B.B.: *Town Planning in Ancient India*, Delhi, 1977.

Devenish, J.A. : *The Bhawans or Garden Palaces*, Allahabad, 1903.

Dwivedi, G.C.: *The Jats: Their Role in the Mughal Empire*, Updated Edition, 2003, Originals, Delhi.

Eintwistle, A.W.: *Braj Culture of Krishna Pilgrimage.*

Elliot and Dowson: *History of India*, Vols. 1-8, Low Price Publications, Delhi.

Fass, Virginia: *Forts of India, Palaces of India.*

Fergusson, James: *History of Indian and Eastern Architecture*, Low Price Publications, Delhi, 1999.

Habib, Irfan: *The Agrarian System of Mughal India*, Bombay, 1963.
Havell, E.B.: *Indian Architecture*, John Murray, 1924.
Irvine, William: *The Later Mughals*, Vols I and II, Low Price Publications, Delhi, 1999.
Joshi, M.C.: *Dig*, Archaeological Survey of India, New Delhi, 1971.
Khadgawat, Nathu Ram: *Rajasthan's Role in the Struggle of 1857*, Jaipur, 1957.
Latif, S.M.: *Agra, Historical and Descriptive*, Calcutta, 1996.
Mishra, R.L.: *The Forts of Rajasthan*, printed by Popular Printers; Kutir Prakashan, Mandawa, (Jhun Jhunu), Rajasthan, 1985.
Pandey, Ram: *Bharatpur upto 1826*, Jaipur, May, 1970.
Qanungo, K.R.: *History of the Jats*, Originals, Delhi, 2003.
Risley, Herbert: *The People of India*, Low Price Publications, Delhi, 2003.
Sahai, Jawala: *Dig, its History and Palaces*, Lahore, 1902.
Sarkar, J.N.: *Fall of the Mughal Empire*, Calcutta, Vol. I (1932), II (1934); *History of Aurangzeb*, Vol. I, III and V, Calcutta, 1924; *Studies in Mughal India*, Calcutta, 1919.
Sardesai: *Panipat Prakaran.*
Sharma, S.R.: *Mughal Empire in India*, Karnataka, 1940.
Sharma, V.D.: *Types of Forts in Rajasthan and their Strategic importance*, A Study in Military Geography, unpublished thesis.
Siddiqui, J.M.: *Aligarh District: A Historical Survey.*
Sidney, Toy: *A History of Fortification*, London, 1966.
Singh, A.P.: *Forts and Fortifications in India*, Agam Kala Prakashan, Delhi, 1987.
Singh, K. Natwar: *Maharaja Suraj Mal*, Radha Krishnan Prakashan, New Delhi, 1985.
Singh, Rajpal: *Rise of the Jat Power*, Harman Publishing House, New Delhi, 1988.
Sircar, D.C.: *Studies in the Geography of Ancient and Medieval India*, Delhi, 1960.
Sompura, O.P.: *Bhartiya Durga Vishanam.*
Thorn, Major William: *Memoirs of War in India.*
Young, P.V.: *Scientific Social Survey and Resesarch.*

***2. Hindi***

Dikshit, G.C.: *Brajendra Vansha Bhaskar*, Agra, Samvat, 1983.
Lal, Sunder: *Bharat Mein Angrezee Rajya*, Onkar Press, Allahabad, 1938.
Vyas, Gopal Prasad: *Braj Vaibhav*, Vrindavan.
Ranawat, M.S.: *Bharatpur Maharaja Jawahar Singh Jat*, Jodhpur, 1973.
Sharma, U.N.: *Jaton Ka Navin Itihas Vol. I*, Jaipur, 1977.
Shastri, Stya Prakash: *Sudan Ratnawali*, Vrindaban.

Singh, Ganga: Yaduvansh, Vol. I, Bharapur, 1967.

Other Books (English)

***3. Urdu Manuscripts***

Suryadwij, Baldev Singh, Tawarikh Bharatpur, 1855-56.

1. *The Columbia Encyclopedia*, edited by William Bridge Water and Elizabeth J. Sherwood, New York, 1950.
2. *Indian Architecture*, Vol. II, Architectonics, edited by M.A. Anathalwar and Alexander Rea, complier, A.V. Thiagaraja Iyer, Indian Book Gallery.
3. *The Gardens of Mughal India*: A History and a Guide, Vikas Publishing House Pvt. Ltd.
4. *Temples of India*, published by Publication Division, Ministry of Information and Broadcasting, Government of India.
5. *Mathura – The Cultural Heritage*, edited by Doris Meth and Srinivasana.
6. *The History and Culture of the Indian People*, Vol. II, 1960; Vol. IV, 1955, Bombay.
7. *Report on the Administration of Bharatpur State (1938-39 A.D.)*, Bharatpur State Press, 1940.

***(Sanskrit Texts)***

1. *Rig - Veda*
2. *Atharva - Veda*
3. *Aitareva Brähmana*
4. *Brihat Samhita*
5. *Padma - Purāna*
6. *Matsya Purāna*

**Gazetteers**

1. K.K. Sehgal, *Rajasthan, District Gazetteer of Bharatpur*, Jaipur, 1971.
2. *Imperial Gazetteer of India* (Provincial series for U.P., (Agra and Oudh) and Rajputana, 2 Volumes, Calcutta, 1908, reprinted, 1989.
3. *The Imperial Gazetteer of India*, Vol. VIII, Oxford, 1908.
4. *Agra Gazetteer*, Allahabad, 1905.
5. D.L. Drake Brockman, *Mathura Gazetteer*, Allahabad, 1911.
6. D.L. Drake Brockman, *Gazetteer of Eastern Rajpurtana*, 1905.
7. F.S. Growse, *Mathura : A District Memoir*, Ahmedabad, 1978. It is Reprint of revised IIIrd edition 1883.